MIRACLES
AMONG
MUSLIMS

—— The Jesus Visions ——

MIRACLES
AMONG
MUSLIMS

—— The Jesus Visions ——

Jesus "…showed Himself alive…"
(Acts 1:3)

CHRISTINE DARG

DESTINY IMAGE JERUSALEM™

An imprint of

DESTINY IMAGE EUROPE™ srl
Via Maiella, 1
66020 San Giovanni Teatino (Ch) - Italy

"Changing the world, one book at a time!"

This book and all other Destiny Image Europe™ books are available at Christian bookstores and distributors worldwide.

To order products, or for any other correspondence:

DESTINY IMAGE EUROPE™ srl
Via Acquacorrente, 6
65123 - Pescara - Italy
Tel. +39 085 4716623 - Fax: +39 085 4716622
E-mail: info@eurodestinyimage.com

Or reach us on the Internet: **www.eurodestinyimage.com**

ISBN 10: 88-89127-38-4
ISBN 13: 978-88-89127-38-4

For Worldwide Distribution. Printed in the U.S.A.

1 2 3 4 5 6 7 8/10 09 08 07 06

Dedication

To secret believers everywhere:

May you draw much strength and courage from these pages.

> *Behold, he standeth behind our wall,*
> *he looketh forth at the windows,*
> *shewing himself through the lattice.*
>
> *My beloved spake, and said unto me,*
> *Rise up, my love, my fair one,*
> *and come away.*
>
> *For, lo, the winter is past,*
> *the rain is over and gone;*
> *The flowers appear on the earth;*
> *the time of the singing of birds is come,*
> *and the voice of the turtledove*
> *is heard in our land....*
>
> *O my dove, that art in the clefts of the rock,*
> *in the secret places of the stairs,*

let me see thy countenance,
let me hear thy voice; for sweet is thy voice,
and thy countenance is comely.

Song of Songs 2:9-14

Acknowledgments

Heartfelt thanks to Pietro Evangelista, publisher of Destiny Image Europe, for having the vision to publish this book worldwide.

Thanks to Michael Little and Victor Oladokun of the Christian Broadcasting Network for permission to quote some testimonies in this volume.

Love and appreciation to my wonderful husband Peter for all of his wisdom and to my sons David and Daniel.

Appreciation also to the Kawar family for helping me to obtain a copy of the "Signs and Wonders" journal mentioned in Chapter 7.

Loving thanks to Shirley Hughes and Peggy Boatwright for their intercessory prayers.

Endorsements

Christine Darg is a modern day Deborah with remarkable boldness. Truly she has trod where many men have been too fearful to venture. Hers has been the reward of seeing signs and wonders amongst a people who have been largely neglected by the bearers of the Gospel. Read this book, and you will be reintroduced to the God of the Bible! It reads like an extension of the Acts of the Apostles and confirms that Jesus is alive today!

Dr. Tony Stone
International Evangelist

Now is the time for such a book. Now is the time for Revelation!…I truly believe this book will prepare many of our precious Muslim viewers to receive the revelation of our Lord Jesus Christ.

Howard Conder
Founder, Revelation TV

Miracles Among Muslims is the most exciting book I have ever read! I highly recommend this supernatural book of Jesus Himself witnessing to Muslims. The wisdom and love contained counter terrorism in the world today!

Pastor Edward Masih
Luton International Church

Christine Darg has followed the Lord's demand to love all people. She has taken the good news of Jesus to the children of both Ishmael and Isaac. She has been the Lord's unique channel of grace, and this book reveals the fruit of love. As one who spends most of his time in the Middle East, I know that a woman is not supposed to be able to do this. But here in this most difficult region of the world, she goes in the strength of Jesus. This book shows what happens when you follow the voice of our Lord.

Canon Andrew P. B. White
President of the Foundation for Relief and
Reconciliation in the Middle East and Anglican Priest for Iraq

Table of Contents

Foreword

As I sit in the center of Baghdad, I hear the bombs and the gunfire, and I endure the intense heat. I am surrounded by my security guards, who carry big guns. Yet there is nowhere in the world I would rather be. Every day people question why I am here. Every day I say because G-d is here like I have never seen him anywhere else.

As I see Jesus in this place, I realize that as Christine Darg says in this book, *Miracles Among Muslims*, G-d has been at work here for a long time. He sent Jonah, the most miserable evangelist in the world, here by submarine transportation. Here King Nebuchadnezzar saw the Son of G-d in the fiery furnace with Shadrach, Meshach, and Abednego. Here Daniel once saw the Son of Man appear over the river Tigris (Daniel 10). My experience is the same as Christine Darg's. I have also seen the glory of G-d here. I too have seen many coming to Jesus because they have seen Him in a vision or dream—not because they have heard drab sermons, but because they have heard and seen Jesus.

On Sunday, as I baptized former Muslims in the former palace of Saddam Hussein, I was acutely aware of the work of the Almighty. We are in a major clash between the light of Christ and the darkness of the evil one, and we know that light always wins.

Christine Darg has been uniquely used by G-d as a channel of His love and wonder to all peoples of the Middle East. She loves both Israelites and the Arab people, and sadly most people do not do this, but this is the work and way of G-d. Her love is shown in this book when Christine quotes the end of the nineteenth chapter of Isaiah—it is the prophetic way of our Lord in this age.

This book is true; it provides a unique look into the ways of G-d in this age. It shows us that G-d is at work in time and space, drawing people to his wonder and love.

That Jesus has enabled Christine to be in the middle of much of this engagement is also a miracle. The Islamic leadership does not usually deal with women, but when the love of Jesus shines through you, people will be drawn to you.

Of this work of G-d, Christine is a unique example, and this is just the beginning—even greater things will happen.

So all the lovers of Jesus must be prepared: in this time, G-d is doing a new thing in a new way in a place where Jesus once walked. Reading this book is a good way to start on this journey. Here we have the story of the work of G-d and not the endeavors of humanity. Read it and you too will see our Lord at work.

Canon Andrew P. B. White
Baghdad, July 2006
President of the Foundation for Relief and
Reconciliation in the Middle East and Anglican Priest for Iraq

Author's Introduction

For God speaketh once, yea twice, yet man perceiveth it not. In a dream, in a vision of the night, when deep sleep falleth upon men, in slumberings upon the bed; Then He openeth the ears of men, and sealeth their instruction (Job 33:14-16).

The risen Lord Jesus is visiting Muslims through dreams and visions in fulfillment of Joel chapter 2, which proclaims that in the Last Days the Holy Spirit will be poured out on all peoples, and young and old alike will experience dreams and visions.

At the same time, on a number of occasions over the past 25 years, the Lord has been directing me to nations through the divine agencies of dreams and visions to preach revivals among the Muslims, specifically in the Holy Land, on the Arabian Peninsula, in Egypt, in the Philippines, and more recently in Iraq.

Since the first edition of *The Jesus Visions*, [the former title of *Miracles Among Muslims*] the phenomena of dreams and visions outpoured in the Middle East have increased—I would almost dare to say, exponentially.

We can hardly keep pace with reports of dreams and visions of our Lord Jesus. An article published in *Mission Frontiers* magazine (March 2001) reported the following, based on questionnaires completed by over 600 Muslims who had placed their faith in Jesus: "Though dreams may play an insignificant role in the conversion decisions of most Westerners, over one-fourth of those surveyed stated quite emphatically that dreams and visions were key in drawing them to Christ and sustained them through difficult times."

A dream can be defined as "a sequence of images passing through a sleeping person's mind," whereas a vision is simply a "mental image" or a religious or mystical experience of a supernatural nature.

Muslims usually describe a typical "Jesus dream" or vision as a peaceful face that they inevitably—somehow—always recognize as Jesus. Often they encounter a compassionate figure in a white robe, who calls them to come to Him. Sometimes His hands and arms are extended wide, or Jesus reaches toward them in love and invitation. Many dreams are preparatory experiences to encourage Muslims to consider the possibility of following Jesus. Other visions or dreams are dramatic experiences of such magnitude that the person knows deeply and without question that he or she is destined to walk the lonely path of faith, even martyrdom, with Jesus.

Why is the Lord favoring Muslims with an extraordinary movement of the Holy Spirit, often bypassing traditional methods of Gospel activity, and aiming straight at their hearts through dreams and visions? I believe it is because this is a *kairos* (preordained time) for the Muslim world to be reached.

Although Muslim lands have been closed to traditional Gospel preaching, it is time for the Lord to fulfill his promise to the patriarch Abraham to bless the descendants of Ishmael. While it is also the set time to favor the descendants of Isaac and Jacob with the restoration of their homeland, God is concurrently remembering his faithful promise to the other side of Abraham's family—the Arabs.

It is difficult to keep pace with the movement of the Holy Spirit in Iraq despite news reports that paint a bleak picture. Behind the scenes the Lord is moving into the vacuum since Saddam's toppling with dramatic power conversions and the planting of many new churches. Iraqis are experiencing dreams and visions of Jesus.

As it is written, "I am sought of them that asked not for Me; I am found of them that sought Me not: I said, Behold Me, behold Me, unto a nation that was not called by My name" (Isaiah 65:1). Truly the Lord Jesus is pleading with the Arabs in the night watches, "Behold Me! Behold Me!"

In Jerusalem a young shopkeeper stopped me in the market to thank me for preaching the Gospel in our open-air banquets at "The Fountain." He said, "I can trust you. I want to show you something." Behind a shelf he was carefully hiding a Bible, which he stroked lovingly and kissed before hiding again. With joy shining from his face, he told me that Jesus now lives in his heart. He had read the entire Bible, including the New Testament, and could not put it down because of the power of its words. But he was tormented by fears of what would happen if he openly declared faith in Yesua al Fadi (Jesus the Savior). One night after praying fervently for three hours, he said the Holy Spirit gave him a dream. He saw a beautiful olive tree, solitary, thriving in the middle of a vast desert. The olive tree pulsated with a heart full of the brightest light he had ever seen. Upon awakening, the man said, "I am so proud of my dream that God gave me, because it confirmed to my heart that my experience with Jesus is true."

I said, "Can I offer a further interpretation of your dream?"

"Yes, please. I am waiting to hear!" the Arab man beamed.

"I believe the olive tree, a great symbol in the Bible, represents yourself in this instance. You are alone in the desert, meaning that you are a pioneer among many isolated believers who are standing alone for Jesus in the Islamic world. But your roots go down deep to receive sustenance from the hidden resources of the Water of life, Jesus, the Holy Spirit, and the Word. The heart you saw on this tree is your own heart, which is filled with the blazing light and glory of Jesus, *the* Light of the World!" I added, "Many others will take refuge under your branches as you trust and grow in the Lord. You have not chosen Him, but He has chosen you that you should bear much fruit for His glory!"

The young man was greatly encouraged. Tears filled his eyes. Part of every believer's ministry in these days of Holy Spirit outpouring should be to interpret the dreams of Muslims and seekers. Many religious persons are indeed zealous for God, but they often need a believer with understanding to explain the Way more adequately. When dreams are granted to divinely chosen persons, the revelations usually begin when their knowledge of God is sketchy. It was so with Abraham, Jacob, and Joseph in the Book of Genesis, and with Solomon in 1 Kings 3:5. Thus many seekers are given major clues about the Lord in their dreams.

And we must be willing and able to teach them with compassion and understanding. A good example of the teaching ministry in the New Testament was the husband-and-wife team of Aquila and Priscilla, who expounded the Gospel to a man who was zealous, but whose knowledge was inaccurate:

> *Apollos...was instructed in the way of the Lord; and being fervent in the Spirit, he spake and taught diligently the things of the Lord, knowing only the baptism of John. And he began to speak boldly in the synagogue: whom when Aquila and Priscilla had heard, they took him unto them, and expounded unto him the way of God more perfectly* (Acts 18:24-26).

One of my dear friends, a former Muslim from India, dreamed that a Cross was moving toward him as it grew brighter and brighter. He was shaken by the dream and received much revelation from it. However, he progressed to a personal faith in Jesus only because a street evangelist also witnessed to him.

We all need an evangelist in our lives. Although one of my earliest childhood memories was a vision of the Lord Jesus, who gloriously healed me, I did not repent of my sins and receive Jesus as Savior until my father explained the Gospel to me several years later. Under great conviction, I pushed forward in one of Daddy's Sunday services to make a public profession of Jesus as Lord and Savior when I was five years old.

A Muslim man from Pakistan wrote to me saying, "I again saw Jesus in my dreams. In the beginning, I was not able to come near to Him, but this time I could touch Him. He gave me a box that I could not open, and then he vanished. Please send me some information on what this dream means."

Even though the Pakistani man had contact with Jesus through dreams, he still needed an evangelist. I wrote to him explaining that the box in his dream represented the treasure trove of Christ—"in whom are hid all the treasures of wisdom and knowledge" (Colossians 2:3). Without revelation of the Holy Spirit, the Pakistani could not open the box. I sent him a Bible and Gospel literature, including the first edition of *The Jesus Visions*, whereupon he answered with a second letter:

> I dreamed that a man was standing at a distance with a book in his hand calling to me with open arms. But I was afraid to go near to him. This dream has happened to me twice this year. I inquired with a dream reader about this dream, but he did not answer me. But, when I studied your book, *The Jesus Visions*, I thought to myself, "He must be Jesus Christ!"

When I share the Gospel, I usually start by asking Muslims if they have experienced a dream about Jesus. It is almost inevitable that they have seen Jesus—amazingly—and so this supernatural phenomenon makes proclaiming the Gospel much easier.

You can argue doctrine with Muslims about the Virgin Birth and the Resurrection all day and make little progress. But when Jesus reveals Himself directly to the souls of men and women, they are easy to convince that He is alive and that He is not just a prophet, but Lord.

I am an evangelist of the empty tomb in Jerusalem. Religion boasts many prophets, but they are all entombed in their graves. Only the tomb of Jesus is empty, because He is alive and very active, especially in the Muslim world.

Furthermore, Jesus is calling many Muslims to Himself in dreams and visions exactly as the prophet Joel predicted would happen in the Last Days. He beckons, "Behold Me," in the night watches. Some are afraid. Some try to ignore Him. But He pursues them relentlessly and mercifully in their dreams and also in open visions.

This book will increase your faith to believe that truly nothing is impossible with God. At a Muslim missions conference there was a photograph of the dry, barren Saudi sands. In the sand a believer had drawn the name "Jesus" in very large letters as a sign of His claim on all nations, even Saudi Arabia. That photo affected me profoundly. It is still working in me deeply today.

Somebody asked me, "Why do you preach to the Muslims? They all believe in God anyway." That person's question displayed ignorance of the Gospel that is all too typical. The Bible teaches that "all have sinned" (Romans 3:23) and that the eternal consequences of our sin is death—"For the wages of sin is death" (Romans 6:23). Furthermore, there is *nothing* that a Jew, Muslim, Hindu, cultural Christian, atheist, or anyone else can do to save himself, but God's love has made a way. "God commendeth His love toward us, in that, while we were yet sinners, Christ died for us. Much more then, being now justified by His blood, we shall be saved from wrath through Him" (Romans 5:8-9). However, we must place our faith in Jesus in order to receive God's complete forgiveness, "That if thou shalt confess with thy mouth the Lord Jesus, and shalt believe in thine heart that God hath raised Him from the dead, thou shalt be saved" (Romans 10:9).

But how will people know the Truth without a preacher? The Lord Himself has been teaching and showing Himself alive to many Muslims—and Jews—through healings, through dreams, and through visions. This book, which is a third edition, continues to chronicle these amazing accounts. May your faith be greatly stirred to realize that our God is not standing by idly in these momentous Last Days, but he is mightily at work pouring out his Spirit through supernatural signs and wonders!

In remarkable ways and on a seemingly unprecedented scale in fulfillment of Bible prophecy, the Lord is showing Himself alive (Acts 1:3).

Christine Darg
Jerusalem

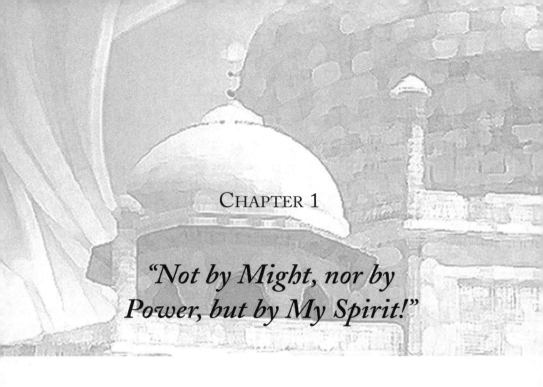

CHAPTER 1

"Not by Might, nor by Power, but by My Spirit!"

And it shall come to pass afterward, that I will pour out My spirit upon all flesh; and your sons and your daughters shall prophesy, your old men shall dream dreams, your young men shall see visions:

And also upon the servants and upon the handmaids in those days will I pour out My Spirit.

And I will shew wonders in the heavens and in the earth, blood, and fire, and pillars of smoke.

The sun shall be turned into darkness, and the moon into blood, before the great and the terrible day of the Lord come.

And it shall come to pass, that whosoever shall call on the name of the Lord shall be delivered (Joel 2:28-32).

God's methods of communicating with us have not changed. Today his main method of communication is through His written Word, the Bible. But because "a picture is worth a thousand words," the Lord also speaks to us in pictures—in dreams and visions—just as He communicated in the Bible to all ranks of people. Through dreams and visions, God sends his children "love letters" of revelation, warning, and guidance. Without a doubt he employed the use of dreams and visions in the Bible from Genesis to Revelation and declared that He would continue to use visions and dreams in the Last Days.

In every age the Lord has granted revelations that have often bypassed the human intellect, even though they are often disregarded as hallucinations. The Bible gives clear-cut guidance to "try the spirits whether they are of God" (1 John 4:1). The revelations in this volume contain nothing contrary to Biblical faith and, in fact, point the way to Jesus and are conformable to Scripture.

A Theophany (literally, Greek for "manifestation of God") or a Christophany ("manifestation of Christ") often occurred in the Old Testament, as when Abraham entertained God for a meal (Genesis 18), or when the Lord appeared in Joshua 5:13-15 as the captain of the heavenly armies.

A Recurring Dream of Jesus Coming in the Clouds

Ibrahim, a former Muslim, experienced supernatural dreams from his childhood resulting from a habit of praising God and asking for guidance before bedtime. A believer gave him a copy of the *Injil* (the Gospels), and he was arrested by Acts 1:10, where angels announced that the ascended Jesus would return in clouds in the same manner in which He departed. Concerning that very verse, Ibrahim had been experiencing recurring dreams such as Muslims are experiencing all over the world:

> I was surprised to see clouds gathering on top of a mountain. After the clouds gathered, two angels dressed in white robes stood on the mountain, and Jesus was standing between them. He left the angels and came to where I was watching. As He approached me, I knelt down, and He laid his hands on my head. With the deep love I felt for Him, I began to repent. The dream was so powerful to me, but in the morning I told no one for fear of what my family would do to me. I remained silent for that year, telling no one what I had experienced.

Ibrahim's reaction is typical of many Muslims who experience supernatural dreams about Jesus. Out of fear of retaliation he kept these wonderful experiences in his heart and pondered them. But the Lord communicated with him the next time in a way to provoke a decision:

> A year later I had the same dream, but this time, Jesus was trying to walk past me. I begged Him not to pass me by, and again I knelt down and repented. But I remained silent because of my fear.
>
> In the third dream, which came yet a year later, as I looked upon the face of Jesus on the mountaintop, He was full of compassion and was smiling down upon me. The two angels were absent this time, but instead a vast multitude of people was present. We were going to where Jesus was, full of peace and joy. The next morning, I sat down to meditate upon this most recent dream. After three years, I finally made an important decision to follow this Jesus who had appeared to me these three times in such overwhelming love. The Lord spoke to me as I read the Gospel of John, "I am the way and the truth and the life. No one comes to the father except through me." This verse provided a bridge between myself and Jesus, and I placed my full trust in Him.

As a minister called by God to the Middle East, I, too, have seen the Lord.

JESUS APPEARED AS A MIDDLE EASTERN MAN

As a very young child, I was very ill and almost died. My Mother said that I had lost all of my hair, suffered from rheumatic fever, and was wasting away. One of my earliest childhood memories was the Lord Jesus appearing to me in an open vision. But unlike some Sunday School pictures of a "Western Jesus," this Christophany was a Middle Eastern man with long, dark, curly hair, brown compassionate eyes, and a Mediterranean complexion. He was wearing a green and white striped Biblical robe. From His appearance, He could have been a Jewish king or an Arab sheik; He was definitely Semitic. I believe He knew that I would one day live in the Bible lands. He said with warm compassion, "You are going to be healed."

I was fearful and awed by the vision and momentarily turned my head to the side. When I looked again, He was gone, but I was healed! To this day I am blessed with vigorous health and I travel throughout the world for Jesus.

JESUS REVEALS HIS WOUNDS IN DREAMS AND VISIONS

Many years later, when I was interceding for the Middle East, I saw the Lord again in a vision. I beheld His sacred wounds, which remain open, so that His stripes and wounds continually heal us by faith. The *stigmata* (marks) Jesus still bears are evidence of the penalty He paid for our sins and sicknesses so that we do not have to bear them. He accomplished a perfect atonement. What a savior! What a healer!

I also saw the whip that was used to tear His flesh when the Roman soldiers scourged Him. To my surprise, in the vision *my* hand was holding the whip. This was because my sins and sicknesses were the cause of His sufferings. We must all recognize ourselves as accomplices in the death of Jesus, because it was our collective sin—the sin of every man, woman, and child that ever lived—that killed Jesus. Mel Gibson, who produced the film *The Passion of the Christ*, understood this concept. In the film, Gibson's hand drove the nails into the Savior at the Cross.

In my vision of the wounded Jesus, He pulled me to Himself with the cords of the whip, and as I embraced Him, His precious blood oozed through my fingers. In the vision, He also placed my hands into His side, pierced by a Roman soldier. He prophesied with great might and urgency into my ear: *"Pray for the sick! Pray for the sick!"* I have not been disobedient to this heavenly vision and have prayed for the sick in every nation to which the Lord has sent me.

As the Holy Spirit continues to pour out visions of the risen Lord, very prominent in these visions are the wounds of His sacrifice on the Cross.

It is notable that "Doubting Thomas" demanded to see the marks of Jesus' suffering and sacrifice. He might have asked for some other sign or proof of the Resurrection, but for Thomas the "print of the nails" and the wounded side would seal his faith. It is also interesting that even though Jesus' death was vindicated and He now exists in a glorified body, the wounds of His crucifixion remain in His body for eternity. They will never be healed over, because the wounds of Jesus are memorials of God's mercy.

Even today Jesus is revealing His sacred wounds to the people of the Middle East. Having been buried alive, an Egyptian child who was rescued testified that a supernatural Man had sustained him—a Man with bloody holes in his hands. There is only one person in the world who fits that description—Jesus Christ of Nazareth.

Visions and Dreams Are Keys to Evangelism

As Islam becomes more conspicuous in the West, Christians are increasingly coming into contact with Muslims. Often we feel inadequate and overwhelmed in our attempts to share our faith. But if we will ask our Muslim acquaintances if they have experienced dreams or visions about Jesus, chances are, more often than not, that we will be amazed at their positive responses. Their dreams are preparatory and often inconclusive, offering clues or "bait" that need an evangelist or a bold believer to explain the way of salvation through faith in Jesus.

When I preached to an Iranian congregation in Germany, many of the believers told me that they had become believers because of supernatural dreams and visions.

A Muslim taxi driver drove me on a 45-minute taxi journey to the airport. He was very talkative, so I asked him if he had ever experienced a dream or vision about Jesus. Most of the Muslims I've approached this way respond positively.

"Strange that you should ask!" he answered, "Just last week I had a dream about a man in a bright robe—Jesus. I was confused about why I should dream about Jesus and not about Mohammed since, after all, I'm a Muslim." The driver's own personal experience in the realm of the supernatural enabled me freely to share the Gospel all the way to the airport and to pray with him. I also gave him a copy of the first edition of this book. The Lord is setting up many such opportunities.

Every church seems to be offering courses on what Muslims believe and how to reach them. It is all rather overwhelming to the average Christian.

But, very simply, Muslims can be reached through yielding to the anointing of the Holy Spirit. The Lord of the Harvest desires to impart to many in these Last Days the gift of evangelism for the unreached Muslim bloc. Effective evangelism will not always be through argument or necessarily through an extensive knowledge of the Koran, but through the power of love and the gifts of the Holy Spirit. It has rightfully been said that arguments produce sceptics, but love makes saints.

Muslims will increasingly figure prominently in prophetic events destined to occur in the end-time generation before the Second Coming of Jesus. Today Muslims are building mosques all over the Western world. There are mosques in Rome, the center of Catholicism, and in Geneva, the citadel of Protestantism. The Queen of England, the head of the Anglican Church, officially cut the ribbon at the opening of the mosque in London's Regent's Park. British Muslims have made no secret of their intention to conquer Britain. In France, Muslims outnumber Protestants two to one. Yet to build a Christian house of worship in an officially Muslim country is a near impossibility. The Muslims are not as cooperative as naive Western leaders.

Mecca Is Not Closed to Jesus

Mecca, the most revered Muslim city, is totally closed to "infidels." As believers in Christ, we are not allowed to set foot in Mecca. Yet Christians once dwelt in Mecca, and Jesus Himself appears in open visions frequently in Mecca and elsewhere in Saudi Arabia! I have been personally informed of numerous testimonies of Muslims who have encountered Jesus in Mecca and who, as a result, have made Him the Lord of their lives.

North Africa was once also a bastion of Christianity. The spread of the Church in the Middle East and North Africa was strong enough to endure crushing persecution from the Roman Empire. Many famous Christian leaders, such as Origen and Augustine, were native sons of the North African church. It was an evangelizing church.

In the lands that first experienced Jesus' preaching, the greatest defeat and reversal in the history of the Christian faith has occurred. Our generation must reclaim lost territory! *However, this will never be accomplished without Holy Ghost evangelism.*

Many devout ambassadors for Christ have labored for years, not only in unripe harvest fields, but also without the promised baptism of the Holy Spirit. Consequently they have seen few results. Yet there are others who preach with an anointing of the Holy Spirit and with the gifts of the Spirit. Veiled women have instantly raised their hands to receive Jesus after witnessing testimonies of healings of breast cancer and other miracles.

Muslim miracles multiply under the ministry of Evangelist Reinhard Bonnke in Africa. After witnessing the Lord's miraculous healing power, many Muslims have boldly testified from Reinard's platform that Jesus is the Son of God. The Lord heals Christians because of the Bible's covenant of healing. He also heals non-Christians because of His mercy—and because healing is a sign and a wonder attesting to the Lordship of Jesus.

I too have been privileged to preach in mass meetings in countries such as Pakistan and in other areas highly populated with Muslims. We rejoice not only that demons that cripple and cause blindness have been subject to us, but that Muslim souls have been transformed and their names written in the Lamb's Book of Life.

It is the bold preaching of the Gospel in love, lifting up Jesus, that opens the eyes of the blind. We rejoice exceedingly at every miracle that confirms the preaching of the Gospel.

God delights in choosing the foolish things of this world to confound the wise. Women in Muslim societies enjoy little authority and practically no rights. For example, the Koran sanctions wife beating in Sura (chapter) 4.

Yet God will anoint not only men but also women to reap a harvest in the House of Islam. He will choose the foolish and weak vessels to confound the wise in Islam.

GOD SENDS A WOMAN EVANGELIST

The God of the universe delights in breaking man's preconceived notions by sometimes choosing even to send a woman. Why he chose me for this end-time task, I don't know, but it is definitely one of the Lord's strategies—probably because we women are not perceived as being much of a threat.

Among women evangelists to the Muslims, "Shaeeda," Jenny de Mayer, is one of my heroines of the faith. Unable to journey any farther than Jeddah with the Gospel in 1920, she prophesied to the gates of Mecca, "How long, O God? How long before the Gospel of Jesus is proclaimed in Mecca?"

Since my childhood I have been fascinated with the Sahara regions of Africa and with the desert peoples of Arabia. The patriarchs of the Bible and Lawrence of Arabia held a fascination for me. The Lord transplanted our family to Jerusalem, where a unique door opened for me to share the Gospel with groups of Israeli soldiers twice a week as they visited Christ Church inside the historic Jaffa Gate. Many signs and wonders happened. A Sephardic woman bent over double was healed on Prophets' Street. A Palestinian *hajji* (one who has made the pilgrimage to Mecca) with terminal lung cancer was healed.

Dreams and visions abounded in our work. I held meetings inside the Old City and was allowed by the Jewish jail keeper to preach in the jail at the Jaffa Gate police station every week. An orthodox Jewish man dressed in the typical ghetto black garb prayed with me not far from the Western (Wailing) Wall. I was privileged to minister to Jewish soldiers visiting Christ Church and content to minister to the wounds of the Jewish. To witness the Jews returning to the Lord in these Last Days is God's greatest vindication. It is proof of the validity of the Scriptures and of the Lord, who declares the end from the beginning and who said that in the Last Days he would regather his ancient people from the four corners of the earth. He promised that he would bring them back to their own land, eventually to call on the Messiah. This, in turn, would unleash dynamic, resurrection life for the Church. What a revival. It will be *the* revival of revivals. Anyone who cherishes in his heart this desire for Israel's redemption truly loves God and His honor.

God also greatly enlarged my heart for the other children of Abraham, the Arabs, whose father was Ishmael, the half-brother of Isaac. By the grace of God, our ministry broke a pattern many years ago. Usually Gospel messengers to the Arabs tend to absorb and reflect the Arabs' offense and enmity against the Jews; and Jewish supporters are not always sympathetic toward the Arabs. Nevertheless, God enlarged my heart with a desire to minister to *all* the children of Abraham— Jews and Arabs, as well as the spiritual seed of Abraham, the former Gentiles who are grafted into the Commonwealth of Israel.

In his wisdom and mercy, the Lord granted me the capacity to love them all equally—Jews, Arabs, and the spiritual seed, our brethren in the Church who are the One New Man, neither Jewish nor Gentile, but a "new species" in Messiah.

Though drawn to the Jews because of their covenant relationship with God, I was equally drawn to the Arabs out of a God-given call. The Lord opened my eyes, and I began to understand that if the Arabs could be won to God, then his holy purposes would be furthered.

I identified with Abraham's prayer that Ishmael might live. I saw the Muslims' desperate need of a Savior because they, like the Jews, are heavily burdened by legalism. Additionally, God gave me a vision of Ishmael and Hagar in Abraham's tent—and their expulsion and their consequent rejection of the faith of Abraham. God furthermore opened a door for me through my friend George Otis to preach every day on the radio throughout the Middle East (the "Voice of Hope" in Lebanon). I received letters from behind the Islamic curtain. I began to preach in Arab homes and in Bedouin tents, in open fields, and even from rooftops in dangerous places.

GOD CALLED ME THROUGH DREAMS TO ISRAEL AND ARABIA

Through an awesome dream, God's audible voice called me from His *Shekinah* (glory). He spoke a warning against anybody trying to harm me, and He voiced a commission that I must stand with the lonely Jews prior to the Messiah's return.

Later, also through a dream, God literally summoned me in an audible voice to Arabia, where I became involved in one of this generation's most supernatural revivals in the territory of a Middle Eastern principality. I was amazed at the Arabs' openness to the Gospel. It was as if they were just dying for someone to reach them with the Good News of the Savior.

The Lord also opened my eyes to give Ishmael a deep drink of Living Water in the sands of Arabia, just as He had opened the eyes of Hagar.

> *And God heard the voice of the lad; and the angel of God called Hagar out of Heaven, and said unto her, "What aileth thee, Hagar? fear not; for God hath heard the voice of the lad where he is. Arise, lift up the lad, and hold him in thine hand; for I will make him a great nation." And God opened her eyes, and she saw a well of water; and she went, and filled the bottle with water, and gave the lad drink* (Genesis 21:17-19).

A NEW COMMISSION TO THE HOUSE OF ISLAM

Although I had begun ministering among the Jews and Muslims of the Middle East, God handed me a new commission in Mombassa, Kenya, to go to the House of Islam in North Africa with the Reinhard Bonnke Christ for all Nations (CfaN) team. I said to God, "How can this be?" But the Lord answered, "If you will be not only obedient but willing to go to the House of Islam, we'll talk later about Israel. It is not yet harvest time for Israel. You must first go to the House of Islam. Will you be not only obedient but willing?"

I quickly adjusted my thinking and said, "Yes." (Sometimes we are like Jonah who was eventually obedient but not willing in his heart.)

"OK, Lord," I said, "but please confirm this call. I'm a wife and a mother and I'm very fair-skinned. You know that hot countries and I don't really mix! You are always calling me to hot countries! And how can this be since I know no man?"

He said, "I will confirm it, 'And blessed is she that believed: for there shall be a performance of those things which were told her from the Lord'" (Luke 1:45).

At the time, I was attending Reinhard Bonnke's meetings in Mombassa, where Islam entered East Africa. After one of the evening meetings, eight Muslim women dressed in black from head to toe wandered onto the grounds. They had missed the sermon. When I saw them, for a moment, I thought I was back in Jerusalem. I was so happy to greet them and asked if I could share about Jesus. I had time to preach only a five-minute sermon because my transportation was ready to depart. Then I asked if they wanted to receive Jesus. They all said, "Yes!" I led them in a very thorough sinner's prayer, renouncing every false way. They said they believed in their hearts that Jesus was raised from the dead (which is something that Muslims are taught not to believe). And they confessed with their mouths that Jesus is Lord. Afterward I exclaimed happily, "How wonderful that all of you have received the Lord Jesus together! Are you friends?"

"No," said one of the women. "We are eight blood sisters." I was amazed. Usually it takes time to build trust before a Muslim will pray the sinner's prayer to receive Jesus. And for eight sisters to confess Jesus all at once—this is most unusual.

That night the Lord said, "What more confirmation do you need that I am calling you to the House of Islam?" I remembered also that eight is the number of new beginnings.

Humanly speaking, I am not qualified to preach to the House of Islam. I am a woman, a despised Westerner educated as a journalist. I am not an Arabist. I cannot read the Koran in the Arab language. But

Reinhard Bonnke also teaches that God has a habit of anointing nonprofessionals to accomplish a task. It's the *un*anointed professionals who often go to a field and accomplish little.

GOD GRANTS TERRITORIAL AUTHORITY

God absolutely delights in granting territorial authority to persons of different nationalities to accomplish his purposes. He will choose a German like Reinhard and give him territorial authority in Africa. He will call African preachers to Britain and the former Soviet Union and elsewhere. He will pick up a girl like me from the American South and plop her down in the Middle East! He will transplant a man like Hudson Taylor from Britain to China, and he will choose a Chinaman like "The Heavenly Man," Brother Yun, to carry the Gospel back to Jerusalem.

God desires to impart the gift of faith for the House of Israel and the House of Islam to all the Church. He is able to reveal Jesus Christ (*Yeshua HaMashiach* in Hebrew) to the chief rabbi or Yesua Al Mesia (*Jesus the Messiah* in Arabic) to the chief mullah in any city whenever He so desires.

Humanly speaking, Islam is formidable. But Christians for too long have used fear or other excuses not to evangelize the Muslims. True, Islam acknowledges Jesus as a prophet, but it denies the very heart of the Gospel. Islam denies the death of Jesus, as well as His Sonship and Resurrection. And since Islam is a universalistic religion with missionary zeal, it will fight back. Therefore we must determine in our hearts not to be fearful if we plan to reach the House of Islam, our Muslim neighbors.

What are our advantages and benefits? Most important of all, we have the name of Jesus, and the authority He has given us in His name. We also have our testimonies and the blood of Jesus: "And they overcame him by the blood of the Lamb, and by the word of their testimony; and they loved not their lives unto the death" (Revelation 12:11).

Do you believe that Jesus is able to win the Muslims? I have found too few in the Church—and especially in the Eastern Church—who believe that the Muslims can be reached and that they will confess

Christ. It is sad to say that the Church is filled with unbelieving believers concerning Islam. But multitudes in Islam can be saved if we learn the strategies of the Holy Spirit.

Filipino Handmaid Fulfills Prophecy

In the Old Testament, a wealthy Syrian general with incurable leprosy was given the key to his healing by a Hebrew slave girl. A similar situation evolved in our day in Saudi Arabia. A Saudi sheik's daughter was dying. No hospital could help her. His vast oil wealth could not save her through the specialists. Then the family's Filipino Christian handmaid humbly asked if she could pray for the girl in the name of Jesus. The daughter was healed, and the family believed and reportedly has a house church in Saudi Arabia, the bastion of Islam. "And upon the handmaids in those days will I pour out my spirit."

Reportedly there have also been a number of dramatic signs in the skies over Muslim nations. From the West African nation of Mali, the following news report was sent to my husband, European and West African Director for the 700 Club TV program.

Face in the "Meteor"

Life in Mali begins to stir before daybreak. By sunrise, the motorbikes, carts, and cars are crowding the two narrow bridges to cross the muddy Niger River from one side of the capital city, Bamako, to the other. One recent morning, those who were awake at 5 A.M. stared at the still-dark sky and the last remaining stars. Vast sections of Bamako have no electricity in the suburbs, and the population is accustomed to finding its way in the gloomy, dusty nights of living on the edge of the great Sahara desert. But on this occasion, there was an unusual light in the heavens.

As the sky grew lighter, suddenly over the horizon people could see a large white light moving south to north. It was surely not a comet or meteor, because it seemed too large and too close, and it was moving at a speed that was easy to follow. Was this some kind of UFO apparition or an aircraft with a searchlight? No one could remember seeing anything like it in his or her lifetime. By daybreak, the light in the sky was the talking point of every conversation in the marketplace, the offices, and schools.

A Malian evangelist began to hear from neighbors who had seen the light that it held another puzzle. More than one eyewitness confirmed that in the light they had clearly discerned the features of a human face. But whose face?

One eyewitness had just watched the Campus Crusade film *Jesus*. For him, the face had the same features—the kind, compassionate expression; the beard; and the countenance of the person in the film. It was, without a doubt, he said, the face of Jesus in that mysterious, inexplicable light streaking across the Muslim nation of Mali.

Mali is the nation that boasts the "ends of the earth" city, Timbuktu. We must wake up and realize that the Gospel is being preached in the uttermost part of the earth, and so soon the Lord Jesus will return!

CHAPTER 2

Miracles in the Holy Land

Muslims are family oriented. They are often at home and have time to chat, unlike frenzied Western lifestyles in which families no longer eat meals together. Arab hospitality commands them to take time with visitors. Often a considerable amount of time in friendship evangelism passes before anyone can be led to Jesus.

On the other hand, we must not be trapped into a mindset that inordinate time will be necessary to develop relationships before some can be saved. I have prayed with some Muslims to receive Jesus after knowing them for only a short time. Sometimes they have prayed with me to receive Jesus on the first encounter. Again, it was because the supernatural was involved.

In Bethlehem, where we held evangelistic services, sometimes Muslims were saved immediately through supernatural signs. With others it took time to build a relationship of trust. But the supernatural was involved in every case. The Holy Spirit and the miraculous played divine roles. Otherwise, Christianity is seen to offer no life, no vitality, and is "just another religion."

Here are some practical examples:

- The Lord graciously used me to lead an Arab patriarch and three of his sons to the Lord. A shopowner in Bethlehem, Abu Yosef, liked to bargain. (I am not a pushover, and the Arabs enjoy that.) Abu Yosef knew I was "religious." (There is a difference, of course, between a real relationship with Jesus and professing religion. He didn't know the difference—not yet, anyway.)

- A relationship of mutual respect developed. Abu Yosef invited us for a meal during the fast month of Ramadan. (After dark, the Muslims feast, but during the daylight they must not eat or drink during Ramadan). Abu Yosef proudly presented all of his sons while his wife served tea and sweets. Arab men are named after their first-born son. He was called *Abu* (father of) *Yosef*. I asked, "Where is Yosef?"

- They hung their heads. Sadly, Abu Yosef said, "He's in prison. He's serving a life sentence for having been involved in a PLO plot in Lebanon when he was just 16 years old. He's already served 10 years. He's 26 years old now."

- He didn't speak with bitterness; he just stated the facts, and I felt the Lord's deep concern. The compassion of the Holy Spirit fell on me for this patriarch and his family.

- We must minister by the anointing. With great compassion, I asked, "Abu Yosef, may I pray for your son to be released from prison?"

- He was very pleased. He trusted me. He said, "Of course, please."

An Unusually Bold Prayer

This is the prayer the Holy Ghost gave me, "Father God, in the name of Jesus Christ, I call Yosef from prison as a sign to this family that Jesus Christ is alive and that Mohammed is still in his grave!"

That was a bold prayer, and it certainly was not premeditated. After we left, I said to my husband, "I can't believe I prayed that prayer."

However, when we follow the Holy Spirit, we are often led to do bold, unexpected things. We become, as it were, another person altogether. As the prophet Samuel informed King Saul, "And the Spirit of the Lord will come upon thee, and thou shalt prophesy... and shalt be turned into another man" (1 Samuel 10:6).

One day I was visiting Bethlehem again. Abu Yosef ran out of his shop, chasing my car. He was ecstatic to see me.

"Christine!" he exclaimed. "Where have you been? I've been waiting to tell you something wonderful." He summoned me into his shop.

"Do you remember when you prayed for my son, Yosef?" he shouted excitedly.

"How could I forget?" I thought to myself.

"Well, here he is!" the father exclaimed and pointed to a man, whom I'd never seen before, sitting in a chair in the back of the shop. It was a miraculous moment to hear the story of how the Israelis had suddenly negotiated a prisoner exchange, and Yosef had been unexpectedly set free.

The Holy Spirit fell on me again, and I boldly said, "Now, Abu Yosef, I want to remind you that your son was brought out of prison in the name of Jesus!"

This answer to prayer was the beginning of Abu Yosef's salvation. He began to believe that Jesus is alive and answers prayer today. And as a result of that one Holy Ghost–directed prayer, another one of his sons became a believer and asked us to baptize him. We did, along with another believer from Kuwait who had been attending my Bethlehem Bible study.

Soon after that, a second son, Munir, followed suit and became a believer. Munir had heard his family speaking about the miracles in the house meetings of "Sister Christine," so Munir assumed I was a Roman Catholic nun! He knew nothing about the various denominations within Christianity or about Christian doctrine. As a Muslim, he had been told that Jesus did not die on the Cross. However, one night Munir dreamed about Jesus dying on the Cross! He also attended a Holy Spirit gathering at our house in Jerusalem. Afterward he prayed with me to receive Jesus. (Munir became a very useful translator in our ministry.) Abu Yosef attended also, in addition to a Christian Arab couple also from Bethlehem, a doctor and his dentist wife.

ARABS FALL DOWN UNDER HOLY SPIRIT POWER

Abu Yosef, a *hajji*, came forward during the ministry time for healing prayer. Though not yet a believer, he was beginning to see the miracles of Jesus. He was touched by the presence of the Lord and fell down under the power of the Holy Spirit! The dentist and his wife, Arab Christians, were softly laughing in the background. I later enquired why they laughed. They said they were not being disrespectful but that they were simply incredulous. They had never seen a *hajji* in a Christian meeting, let alone one coming forward for prayer for healing in the name of Jesus!

We Christians in the West have become almost jaded in our attitudes when we see people fall down under the power of the Holy Spirit. But this sign and wonder definitely affected Abu Yosef and intrigued his sons who became believers. To this day, they still talk about it.

Many years later, our ministry held a healing service in a hotel in Acre, in northern Israel, and Arabs who attended also fell down under the power of the Holy Spirit when we prayed for them. We would never attempt to force people from any culture to fall down. But they were overcome by the presence of the Lord.

Still another time during a healing meeting on the summit of the Mount of Olives, the *kavod* (glory, heaviness) anointing of the Holy Spirit was so powerful that many people could not stand. Our Muslim hosts carried people out of The Tent, a venue that we had hired. A Muslim named Mohammed put his faith in Jesus that night as a result of the sign ministry of people falling down under the power of God.

Mohammed told me he had never seen a sign and a wonder like that in a mosque.

Remember, the Lord talks to us in pictures, dreams, and visions. The Holy Spirit, in fact, opened doors for me to preach in Bethlehem through a dream that he gave to an Arab.

One day I was passing through Bethlehem with a co-evangelist. We had not visited Bethlehem for several weeks because of the unrest that preceded the first *intifada*. We stopped in a restaurant for lunch, and a Christian Arab named Elijah rushed in to say, "Christine, I had a dream early this morning that you were coming to Bethlehem and that you came to my house to minister." This was the influence of the Holy Spirit. My friend and I went to his house right away and held an impromptu Gospel meeting among the mother, sisters, brothers, and neighbors—preaching Christ and praying for the sick. That meeting took place only because of a dream given by the Lord. A woman who had not been able to conceive a child because of many miscarriages received power from the Lord to have a baby. Other healings were reported back to me, and I was greatly encouraged that the Arabs were wide open to the movement of the Holy Spirit!

God's hand was on Abu Yosef's entire family in a remarkable way. We have noticed that there are certain families that are especially favored as forerunners in the coming great revival in Islamic nations. This next story illustrates how the Holy Spirit works, with his gifts, to draw a Muslim into the Kingdom of God. (Every conversation, every encounter, can be a milestone in a person's journey to salvation.)

Another of Abu Yosef's sons, Daoud, found us holding a Bible study in a restaurant on another occasion. Daoud sounded desperate when he said to me, "Sister Christine, I've got to talk to you at once. Every night for the past seven nights I've had the same dream. It's a terrible nightmare. At exactly 2 A.M. I awake with the thought that someone is going to kill me with a knife."

In a flash, the Holy Spirit gave me the key to win him for the Lord. (We should ask the Lord to give us the key to people's hearts.) This is what the Holy Spirit said:

"Those dreams are from the devil. You know in your heart that you need to accept Jesus as your Lord and Savior, like your brothers have done, but you are afraid. (For a Muslim, conversion can mean death—even from the hands of family members.)

"A spirit of death, a spirit of murder, is intimidating you. But we will take authority over that spirit and bind it in the name of Jesus, and you will never be troubled with it again. You also need to pray now to receive Jesus so that you will be assured of the protection of His name and His blood, as a rightful Child of God."

On the spot, Daoud bowed his head and prayed the sinner's prayer to receive Jesus into his troubled heart. We also took authority over the spirit of death, and the nightmares ceased.

The manner in which the patriarch Abu Yosef finally gave his heart to the Lord was dramatic, and again, the supernatural was involved. He had, at one point, called a family council to discuss killing Munir, who was now serving as my interpreter! Abu Yosef was old enough to be my father, and he often told his family that I was their adopted daughter. But now he was angry with me. (His wife respected me and had allowed me to pray with her for various needs.)

DREAMS ARE GOD'S "M. O."

One night Abu Yosef experienced a troubling dream about me. Dreams are God's "m.o." (method of operation) to speak directly to somebody with a personal communication. In this dream Abu Yosef returned to Jordan to his former work place. I came into his office. In his dream, I was an old woman. My hair was white. He was shocked to see me in that condition, and he cried out, "What has happened to you? You are like a daughter to me. Whatever it is that you need, I will help you."

Actually, I needed no help, but the Holy Spirit used the empathetic dream to increase my favor with Abu Yosef. In his mind, after the dream, instead of being upset with me, he felt somehow responsible for my welfare, like a father. When he heard that I was in Bethlehem, he insisted that I come to dinner at their house. He seemed no longer upset with me for having evangelized his family.

FASTING REQUIRED FOR REVIVAL

The invitation came at the conclusion of a fast to win souls. A prayerful friend also fasted to undergird my visit. I believe our fasts were instrumental in the winning of his soul: "This kind can come forth by nothing, but by prayer and fasting" (Mark 9:29).

Fasting therefore is a very powerful key to win Muslims to Jesus. For centuries, Islam's principality has enjoyed untold millions of Muslims fasting to please it religiously during the month of Ramadan. (And some Christians naively think they can forfeit chocolate for a day and watch that entrenched spirit yield to Messiah!) The Lord is calling His people to accomplish three-day "Esther crisis" fasts, 40-day fasts, and all sorts of corporate "relay fasts" to believe for the release of the captives.

During the meal, Abu Yosef could only talk about the supernatural dream he had experienced about me. This preparation of his heart through a dream put him in a spiritual mood. God sends us dreams to communicate with us, just as a kindergarten teacher instructs children with pictures and storybooks. Never forget that God used a dream to rebuke Abimelech for stealing Abraham's wife. He prepared Joseph in a childhood dream to save his people in Egypt many years later. God sent Peter and Paul to the Gentiles through dreams and visions.

After dinner, we sat on a balcony overlooking Bethlehem while the womenfolk scurried about to serve Arabic coffee. It is unusual to talk privately with anyone in an Arabic family, because the other family members are ever-present, but God is sovereign, and for ten divine minutes everyone was distracted with clearing up dishes and making coffee. Even the sons and grandchildren seemed mysteriously to evaporate. At that choice moment, Abu Yosef looked at me and said that he had a serious heart problem that probably required an operation. He was suffering from shortness of breath.

This patriarch exuded dignity and a certain presence. I was a guest in his domain. The utmost politeness and deference to his feelings were in order.

But this is the response that the Holy Spirit gave me, and I believe it is a key to Islamic evangelism:

"I will surely pray for your heart to be healed, in Jesus' name," I said, "but before I do that, may I ask you a question?"

"Yes," he said emphatically.

"Abu Yosef," I ventured, "it is one thing to pray for your heart and for you to be healed. But what good would it do if your body is healed and yet you go to hell without assurance of salvation? Tell me. When you go to the mosque, you wash your hands and your feet, but how do you wash your heart?

He was listening very carefully.

I continued, "It would be impossible for you to cleanse your heart, because you would have to cut yourself open to remove your heart and to clean it, just as you clean your hands and your feet before worshipping God. It is impossible for you to wash your own heart, isn't it?"

"Yes," he said emphatically.

"But God has made a way for your heart to be cleansed from all sins and for us to be acceptable in God's sight. The red blood of Jesus by faith washes our dirty hearts and makes them clean and white as snow, acceptable to a holy God."

(That phrase is very powerful. The Muslims often speak of somebody having a "white heart," meaning a good heart.)

"This is how we obtain a white heart," I said, "a cleansed heart: Jesus died on the Cross to make an atonement for our sins. The *Injil* [the New Testament] teaches that after Jesus ascended to Heaven, He took His own blood to Heaven and sprinkled it there on the mercy seat of God. Abu Yosef, can there be anything dead in Heaven?"

"No," he said.

"The blood of Jesus is in Heaven now and there is life in the blood of Jesus. Today there is still power in the blood of Jesus. When you look to Jesus by faith, His blood is able to cleanse you from all of your sins."

There was silence as Abu Yosef pondered what I was saying. It was as if we were enveloped in a time warp. I was amazed and awed that nobody had interrupted us.

"Would you like to pray with me right now to receive Jesus as your Lord and Savior and to have His blood cleanse your heart?"

"Yes." He was still emphatic.

"I will also pray for the Lord to heal your heart physically," I added.

This is the prayer that Abu Yosef repeated:

"Dear Father in Heaven, I repent of all my sins. I renounce all false, dead religion. I now call on the name of the Lord Jesus Christ, for You have promised in the Bible that all who call on His name shall be saved. I believe in my heart that You raised Jesus from the dead, and I now say with my mouth that Jesus is Lord! Thank You that his blood is cleansing me now, in Jesus' name. Amen."

"Abu Yosef, do you realize what you have done, that you now believe in Jesus Christ as your Savior?"

"Yes!" he said.

Then I prayed for his physical healing, because healing is the children's bread, and Abu Josef had just become a child of God through Jesus Christ! (His doctor confirmed that he was healed.)

After the prayer time, I asked Abu Yosef again, "Do you realize what you have just done?"

"Yes!" he said decisively. He had a strong-willed personality and could never be coerced to do anything.

"You now belong to Jesus?"

"Yes!" Oh, it was marvelous to hear such an answer to my prayers and fasts.

Suddenly, a riotous argument broke out between two neighboring families. Abu Yosef was distracted by the shouting and ran to the balcony rail to see what was happening. Then the women brought out demitasse cups of sweet Arabic coffee and the conversation was finished. God had provided those ten vital minutes of peace during which Abu Yosef received Jesus.

I gave him an Arabic New Testament dedicated with these words: "To Abu Yosef, my father, who is also now my brother but also my son in Jesus." Later, I was meditating and wondering if Abu Yosef was reading the New Testament I had given him. Early one morning, I experienced a dream about him. It was as if the Holy Spirit was assuring me that Abu Yosef was still standing for the Lord. I saw him healed of the heart condition and back in his souvenir shop. But this time, in the dream, he was selling cakes to everybody. The white icing was decorated with the words, "Jesus is the Answer."

Years later, Abu Yosef died, having lived out a full life span. The Lord gave me a poignant night vision about this pioneer out of Islam seated in heaven.

In my dream, Abu Yosef was sitting alone in a white robe and *kifiyeh* (headdress) at a table drinking what looked like Arabic coffee in heaven. He spoke to me and said, "Well, Christine, I am happy to be here, but I miss many of my own people. Go and bring more of my people into the Kingdom!" I have never forgotten this dream, and the Lord has used it to spur me onward.

A MODERN CHRISTMAS MIRACLE

The testimony of an Arab brother whom the author knew well for almost two decades is another example of the merciful outpouring of the Holy Spirit in the Middle East through dreams and visions. For many years before his death, Ali was a watchman on the Mount of

Olives, and he became one of the most precious prayer partners of our ministry.

Many times Ali interceded for us when we were preaching in dangerous places. He patiently served Jesus through many persecutions and deep heartaches. But the Lord, with the gifts of many dreams and visions, consoled him. Though he lived in a humble abode and was misunderstood by most of his family, this dear brother surely received a great welcome in heaven! A few years ago, I experienced a dream in which I saw this brother drowning and calling for help. I telephoned him to learn that he had become paralyzed. A ministry associate and I visited him and commanded him to walk again in the name of Jesus. He was healed in order to continue his ministry of intercession. The Lord encouraged him with words from the Bible and with dreams and impressions. This is Ali's amazing story, which he shared with me many times:

> I am the unknown soldier of Jesus. The Lord is my shepherd; I shall not want. I believe I was always looking for the Lord, but I didn't know how to find Him. Once I visited Jesus' empty Garden Tomb in Jerusalem because in my heart I was seeking the Lord. I did not find Him, but He found me! I did not choose Him, but He chose me!
>
> When I was working in a hotel, I was overdrinking and under a lot of financial pressure, and one night at 7 P.M. as I was sitting at the bar, I collapsed and suffered a severe nervous breakdown. I was put in the intensive care ward in Bethlehem, and my life was sustained by an intravenous drip, when suddenly, after I had spent forty days in a coma, on Christmas Eve, there was what I can only describe as an earthquake in the hospital. I saw the wall open, and a beautiful man walked into the ward and stood by my bedside. He was the most handsome man I had ever seen. This man was Jesus.
>
> Suddenly, I had a vision of Jesus brighter than the sun and the moon and all the stars combined; and I saw colors that I've never seen on earth. At first I thought He was Joseph,

because the holy book of my religion, the Koran, said that Joseph was the most beautiful man who had ever lived.

But Jesus called me by my name twice in Arabic, and He said to me, "Ali, Ali, I am Jesus; you have not chosen Me, but I have chosen you!"

He laid his hand on my shoulder, and He spoke supernatural messages to me in about twelve or fourteen different languages, and then He spoke to me in Arabic again and said that I was healed.

Immediately I sat up and pulled the drip out of my arm. My doctor and nurses looked at me like they had seen a ghost, because I was almost like Lazarus who was raised from the dead! That was thirty years ago, and I am still walking with the Lord Jesus. When my family took me home, I told them about Jesus, but my brothers stole everything from me. I suffered many things, but the fellowship of Jesus was greater than their hate.

The Lord continues to speak to me in dreams and visions. In a very important vision in 1987, before the [first] *intifada*, He appeared to me with the Bible in His hand and told me that many troubles were coming, but that I would overcome by the words in the Book. Amen.

In 1993, I had a dream in which I found a cross buried in a hole in the ground, which I uncovered. I believe the meaning of this dream is that religion has carried the Cross, but we must lift up the Cross of Jesus, for it is the power of God!

SIGNS AND WONDERS AT ALI'S DEATH

"Precious in the sight of the Lord is the death of His saints" (Psalms 116:15). Ali, of blessed memory, died after the second edition of this book was published. I have never known a person from a Muslim background who enjoyed so many visions and dreams as did Ali. His death made a profound impression on his family and neighbors. His son, who was with him when Ali passed to glory, gave this testimony:

I have never seen a man die like my father died. He was lying on his bed and began to laugh with joy as he looked up, and then he was gone. His white hair and moustache returned to black, the way he looked as a young man. The room was filled with a beautiful fragrance. With these signs, God was telling us what a special man our father was.

It had always been a pleasure to be in a prayer meeting with Ali, who to me was a modern saint and Christian pioneer from the House of Islam. He sometimes prayed and prophesied very dramatically, as did Agabus the prophet in Acts 21:11. He would suddenly take a chain (a family heirloom from his father's old plough) off of the wall, and with his hands he would fervently manipulate it as an "object lesson" when he bound satan in prayer in Jesus' name.

JESUS DREAM OF THE LATE PLO CHIEF YASSER ARAFAT

Bible teacher R. T. Kendall met often with Yasser Arafat. "I began praying for Arafat daily over 22 years ago," Kendall testified, "but I never expected to meet him. I did it because the Holy Spirit laid him on my heart and gave me a love for him. I don't know if Yasser Arafat ever felt unconditional love from many people, especially from the West, but I wanted him to feel it from me. I had one goal: to be Jesus to him."

Kendall, minister at London's Westminster Chapel for 25 years, said he began praying for Arafat daily after hearing the cross-carrying evangelist Arthur Blessitt talk about his visit with the head of the Palestinian Liberation Organization. Blessitt said he knew for a fact that Arafat had experienced dreams about Jesus.

Kendall related on his Web site (rtkendallministries.com) that Arafat told Kendall that he experienced a dream in which, in Arafat's words, "A lamb led me to Bethlehem. There I saw the Virgin Mary holding Jesus. I kissed Jesus. When I woke up, I was so moved that I ordered a lamb to be slaughtered and taken to the priests at the Church of the Nativity in Bethlehem for them to have a feast."

Kendall then reportedly said to Arafat, "I want you to confess that Jesus actually died on the Cross for your sins. Not that he was delivered from the Cross, but that Jesus actually died."

When the Arab translator objected, Kendall says, "Arafat lifted his hand to the translator to suggest that it was all right for me to continue."

After he explained to Arafat the benefits of becoming a Christian, the translator objected again to Kendall's call for conversion. "I replied, 'I am only trying to get him to go public with what he already believes.' I said to Arafat, 'Nothing else has worked. Peace [in the Middle East] will not come through a military or political solution.'" Only the Prince of Peace, Jesus, can bring ultimate peace!

My friend, the Rev. Andrew White, a canon of the Coventry Cathedral in England and former envoy of the archbishop of Canterbury to the Middle East, arranged Kendall's meetings with Arafat. Before Arafat died, Kendall made another trip to present him with a copy of Mel Gibson's film *The Passion of the Christ*. This trip was made public by the Palestinian press, which was allowed into Arafat's Ramallah compound and took photos. Dr. Saeb Erekat, the Palestinian spokesman, translated the subtitles of the movie as it was shown.

> Dr. Erekat asked me afterward if I noticed that President Arafat wept a number of times as he watched. I could hear him weeping but did not look at him except to whisper a few comments about the film as it proceeded. He watched the entire film along with about 30 members of the PLO and Cabinet. At the end of the film I asked President Arafat if I could pray with him. After all in the room left, except for Dr. Erekat, whom I asked to remain. I prayed with him. He made it clear he welcomed this. My sole motive in showing the film was pastoral and evangelistic. I have stressed to Arafat again and again that Jesus *died on the Cross*—and was not delivered from dying on the Cross. I felt that Mel Gibson's film was therefore a potential vehicle of the Holy Spirit to drive this fact home. In my prayer (during which he took

my hand and held it tight) I said, "Heavenly Father, I thank you for the high privilege of showing this film to President Arafat. I pray that you will apply the truth of this film by your Holy Spirit. Make both of us thankful that Jesus died on the Cross for our sins," among other things. We had lunch, he allowed me to pray for all the PLO, walked me out, and kissed me good-bye.

There is no record that Mr. Arafat publicly confessed Jesus or showed fruits of repentance before he died, but the God of Israel in a dream reportedly confronted a terrorist leader in the Middle East—a leader of Hamas in Hebron! This report is from a truthful, reputable high-level official who works in the Middle East. In the dream, the God of Israel upbraided the terrorist and said that it would not go well with his people if the Hamas leader continued to engage in terrorism, murder, and mayhem against the restored ancient people of God. My source told me that this former Hamas leader had to be airlifted out of his hometown as a result of his change of heart.

CHAPTER 3

Let Ishmael Live!

Then Abraham fell upon his face, and laughed, and said in his heart, Shall a child be born unto him that is an hundred years old? and shall Sarah, that is ninety years old, bear?

And Abraham said unto God, O that Ishmael might live before Thee! (Genesis 17:17-18)

In this hour, God is surely answering the prayer of his friend Abraham, "O that Ishmael might live!"

Ishmael was the patriarch of the Arabs. And in the Arab world, the Lord has been showing the New Testament to many by visions of something like a giant TV screen in the night. Many have beheld and handled the Lord's wounded hands and feet. Others have seen the last 24 hours of His life. They have been granted compelling visions and dreams of His agonizing prayer in the Garden, and of the Crucifixion, death, burial, and Resurrection. They wake up convinced that Jesus is not just a prophet but also the Son of God.

Mention visions and dreams, however, and some people react like they've seen a ghost! This is ridiculous because there are plenty of visions in our spiritual manual, the Bible.

- Concerning the birth and safety of the baby Jesus, Mary and Joseph were guided continually through visions and dreams.

- The Apostle Paul was converted and commissioned by a vision; he received the Macedonian call in a night vision.

- The Apostle Peter preached the glorious Gospel to the Gentiles because of instructions given in a trance-like vision.

- John, the beloved disciple, received the Book of the Revelation by visions.

Furthermore, the Scriptures specifically predict that visions and dreams will characterize the end-time move of the Holy Spirit: "And afterward, I will pour out My Spirit on all people. Your sons and daughters will prophesy, your old men will dream dreams, your young men will see visions" (Joel 2:28).

God may surprise your theological concepts if in your mind you confine the Holy Spirit in a box. Throughout the world, the Holy Spirit is moving in the realms of dreams and visions, especially in the most unevangelized area on the map known as the "10/40 window" that stretches from North Africa to Asia.

When the Holy Spirit genuinely inspires visions, they glorify God and bear fruit for the Lord's kingdom. However, we must emphasize that these wonderful visions and dreams are *sovereign* works of *grace*. While the overriding sovereignty of God is one of the most blessed and comforting doctrines, nevertheless the lost peoples of this world still need the glorious Gospel preached to them. The Lord certainly has not abandoned the method of the "foolishness of preaching" (1 Corinthians 1:18-21).

When the Holy Spirit was outpoured at Pentecost, people believed en masse. The day is still coming when the glory of God will be revealed again in the Middle East, and there will be a mass revelation of

Christ as Lord, Savior, Messiah, the Last Word. The Holy Spirit is God's greatest weapon of mass conversions!

There have been and continue to be harbingers of this coming Harvest in the Middle East. Indeed, what the Lord has already performed, He is well able to do again!

SALVATION FOR THE SHAZLIS

The life story of British explorer Sir Richard Burton documents one of the most amazing events of a mass movement to Jesus in the nineteenth century—not through missionaries, books, Bible distribution, or pamphlets but through the divine agencies of dreams and visions! Incredible as it may seem, what the Lord has done before, He is well able to do again!

This particular movement of the Holy Spirit began in the year 1868 in Damascus amongst the Shazli sect of Islam, who were messianic in nature. Jesus appeared separately to them through similar dreams. Some of the dreams pointed out a simple priest holding a lantern; this priest would teach the Shazlis the truth. The Holy Spirit had so encouraged them to follow the Good Shepherd, and they were so filled with a happiness they had never before experienced, that they were hardly dissuaded from proclaiming Christ in the streets!

We quote from a biography of Burton, "What originally had seemed like no more than a few hundred... Arabs seeking a Savior... quickly assumed the proportions of a major heresy. Some 25,000 Shazlis were now reported ready for baptism.... Events now ran out of control for the Shazlis and for Burton."[1]

The account relates how Sir Richard had rather naively hoped that Jerusalem's Latin patriarch would baptize all 25,000 Shazlis and assist in their safe resettlement!

But apparently it was not politically or "religiously" correct for these Muslims to change their religion. The patriarch reported the extraordinary phenomenon to the authorities at Damascus, and that action brought a swift end to the Shazli saga.

"In the end," writes the author, "the British embassy at Constantinople, the Latin patriarch in Jerusalem and [high-ranking Turks] all had a role in betraying the converts." Many were cruelly martyred.

The question must be asked: if the Holy Spirit moved powerfully again in the Middle East and 25,000 or more Muslims in a city desired with all of their hearts to turn to Jesus, would the institutional Church welcome them today? Or would church leaders again do the "politically correct" thing and betray the believers?

JESUS VERIFIES HIS CRUCIFIXION TO MUSLIMS

The story of Al-'Uris is another historical case in point of great significance. He was a person associated with the family of Saladin, the famous Muslim warrior, and Ayyubid, sultan of Egypt and the great opponent of the Crusaders. In the journals of the Ayyubids and their conflicts with the Crusaders, Muslim history records an extremely significant dream of Al-'Uris, one which sounds similar to the above account of the Shazlis!

> Al-'Uris saw in his sleep Christ Jesus, Son of Mary, who seemed to turn his face toward him from Heaven. Al-'Uris asked him, "Did the crucifixion really happen?" Jesus said, "Yes, the crucifixion really happened." Al-'Uris then related his dream to an interpreter, who said, "The man who saw this dream shall be crucified. For Jesus is infallible and can speak only the truth, yet the crucifixion he spoke of cannot refer to his own, because the Glorious Qur'an specifically states that Jesus was not crucified or killed. Accordingly, this must refer to the dreamer, and it is he who shall be crucified." The matter turned out as the interpreter said.[2]

Tragically, Al-'Uris was brutally killed because Jesus tried to communicate with him the truth concerning His death and Resurrection. Perhaps Al-'Uris did trust in Jesus as his personal Savior after all; he was, in fact, crucified for relating this dream.

Similar betrayal and suffering echo in the experiences of present-day martyrs. Imagine confronting the living God and knowing the truth of the Gospel with absolute certainty. Your first instinct might be to "shout it from the housetops." But what would the reaction of a neighbor or relative be to your declaration? We cannot be sure how many countless people have experienced the reality of Jesus through visions and divine revelation, but there are surely a great many who tremble at the consequences of publicly admitting such a momentous, life-changing encounter.

In a more secure environment, these stories circulate freely. Arabs living in Israel, the only democracy in the Middle East, frequently feel relatively free to share their remarkable dreams and visions. A Palestinian acquaintance named Mufeed, for example, openly described how he had met the Lord one night while walking along the dusty road of a refugee camp. No Christian missionary had witnessed to him! Jesus simply appeared to him in a halo of light and said, "I am Jesus. Follow me."

WOMAN IS PRE-EVANGELIZED IN DREAM BY JESUS

Many women are also meeting the Lord through supernatural circumstances. A Bible worker in the "Community of Reconciliation," an evangelical organization in Jerusalem that ministers to both Jews and Arabs, wrote in the organization's journal that she had visited an Arab woman five times and was never able to say anything significant about Jesus. The woman, Halima, was 28 years old, divorced and disappointed with life. Soon she would be yoked in marriage to a man who was 50 years old; thus she would be provided for again and would no longer pose a threat to the family honor as a divorced single mother.

After a meal that broke the fast during the month of Ramadan, the Bible worker sat alone for a while with Halima. This Christian worker testified how Jesus had healed her from many inner wounds. Halima also suffered in her soul. And then, to the Christian's amazement, Halima shared a dream she had experienced:

"I saw a man who was dressed in white and also had white hair. He invited me to look out of a window and I saw a shining green meadow. The man in white had water, too, which was very clear and clean. He gave me to drink some of it. I have never tasted such good water before."

The Bible woman was amazed! Jesus had already revealed much about Himself in Halima's dream! For example, in the Book of Revelation, Jesus is described as a man in white garments with white hair; and in Psalm 23 and in John 10, Jesus is the Good Shepherd who leads his sheep to peaceful, green meadows. In John 4, He offers a woman His own thirst-quenching water of life. The woman evangelist had wondered how she could share Jesus, and here He Himself had already prepared Halima to hear and receive the Gospel!

Another acquaintance of mine, Magid, was performing daily prayers in the cemetery below the Golden Gate near the Temple Mount. He testified in one of my meetings that the voice of our Lord Jesus Christ called him audibly: "Magid! I am the only Savior. Trust Me."

Yosuf, a surly post office employee, seemed an unlikely candidate to embrace the Good News. But I have learned never to underestimate the power of the Holy Spirit. This miserable-looking man, after being invited to our Bible study, gladly prayed the sinner's prayer to receive Jesus as Savior and as the sacrifice for all his sins.

What nobody knew was that Yosuf had already been prepared by a dream years before. In fact, when Yosuf was a young boy, he experienced a dream of Jesus' holy and bruised body lying in the garden tomb—dead, buried, and shrouded. Years later I was able to offer this explanation to him: "Yosuf, the Lord wanted you to know that He *died* for your sins."

You see, the religious teaching under which Yosuf was brought up denies that Jesus died for the sins of the world. His comprehension was limited to the idea that Jesus was spirited away to Heaven, that He was too good to die, and that a vile sinner, Judas, died on the Cross instead. But the Islamic deviation from the Gospel accounts steals the very heart of the Gospel. If Jesus did not die, we don't have a Savior who was God's holy sacrifice and substitute for our sins. If Jesus has not ascended to the Father and is not seated at the right hand of the

Almighty, then we no longer have an intercessor and an advocate who can mediate as high priest on our behalf.

The Good News is that Jesus *did* die on the Cross to pay the penalty for the sins of the world! And if we will believe in our hearts that God raised Him from the dead and dare to confess with our mouths that Jesus is Lord, the Bible assures us that we shall be saved!

> *For Moses describeth the righteousness which is of the law, That the man which doeth those things shall live by them. But the righteousness which is of faith speaketh on this wise, Say not in thine heart, Who shall ascend into Heaven? (that is, to bring Christ down from above:) Or, Who shall descend into the deep? (that is, to bring up Christ again from the dead.) But what saith it? The word is nigh thee, even in thy mouth, and in thy heart: that is, the word of faith, which we preach; That if thou shalt confess with thy mouth the Lord Jesus, and shalt believe in thine heart that God hath raised Him from the dead, thou shalt be saved. For with the heart man believeth unto righteousness; and with the mouth confession is made unto salvation. For the scripture saith, Whosoever believeth on him shall not be ashamed. For there is no difference between the Jew and the Greek: for the same Lord over all is rich unto all that call upon him. For whosoever shall call upon the name of the Lord shall be saved* (Romans 10:5-13).

Jesus became "the author of eternal salvation" (Hebrews 5:9). God uniquely honored Him by choosing him to die as the Atonement sacrifice for the world. Jesus has triumphed, He has presented Himself the sacrificial Lamb of God, and His sinless blood is 100 percent pure to cover the transgressions of the entire race of mankind.

Yosuf's countenance was always surly. One day I said to myself, "Anybody who looks that miserable needs to hear the Good News!" So I plucked up courage and invited this morose and unpleasant man to our Wednesday night Cross Cultural Bible Study at Christ Church inside Jerusalem's Jaffa Gate.

To my utter amazement and surprise, he thanked me for the invitation and came to the meeting. He listened intently. Afterward, during personal ministry time, he said sheepishly, "I can't believe that you invited me to church, because I am a Muslim." But I've always tried to follow the Apostle Paul's example of becoming all things to all people so as to win some. I think Paul's is one of the most brilliant and adventurous evangelistic tactics, and I never tire of trying to be all things to all people to win some to Him.

So I said delightedly, "I'm thrilled that you came. Jesus loves all the people of Jerusalem, including the Muslims. Jesus died for you, too." This genuine expression of acceptance and love reached deep into Yosuf's spirit. He smiled for the first time. His face looked entirely different. A couple of days later, I was in the church's coffee shop. He spotted me and came in. He ventured, "I had a dream when I was six years old about Jesus. Can you tell me the meaning of it?" What a supernatural setup by God for this man's salvation! I love such a challenge, because you never know what inspiration the Holy Spirit might give. Walking with the Lord is a constant adventure.

I said, "I can't tell you the interpretation, but the Holy Spirit can, and I will ask Him to give it to me!" I sat poised to listen.

"OK," he said, "this was the dream. I saw Jesus' face when he was buried in the tomb. I was only six years old, but I'll never forget that face and the light that shone from it. I don't know how I knew that it was Jesus, but I have just always known in my heart that it was Jesus."

"Yosuf," I said excitedly, but gently, "I already know why you were given that specific dream. The Holy Spirit shows me that it's because Muslims don't believe that Jesus died on the Cross and was buried. You have been taught to believe that God spirited Jesus off to Heaven and allowed someone else to die in his place. You have been taught that Jesus was too good to die. But his death, burial, and resurrection are the heart of the Gospel! *Jesus had to die* so that He could make atonement, a substitutionary death, for you and for me. God gave you that dream so that you would know that Jesus *did* die for your sins. He *had* to die in order to complete your salvation. The Bible also assures us that He was resurrected and that over five hundred witnesses saw Him. Would you like to pray to receive Jesus as your Lord?"

Yosuf said yes, and right there in the coffee shop, he bowed his head, prayed the sinner's prayer, said that he believed in his heart that God raised Jesus from the dead, and confessed with his mouth that Jesus is Lord.

OUTPOURING OF VISIONS TO MULLAHS

Like an addendum to the Book of the Acts of the Holy Spirit, the Spirit of God performed a most unusual marvel in southeastern Europe. God began to speak in visions and dreams to 24 mullahs[3] who live near the Bulgarian border with Turkey. During these manifestations, Jesus typically said, "I am Jesus Christ the Messiah. You must repent of your sins and put your faith in me to be forgiven."

None of the mullahs knew anything about the experiences of the others who were also receiving visitations from the Lord. But each of them obeyed the vision of Jesus and faithfully proclaimed what they had seen and heard. Their congregations began to seek God through His Son Jesus, repenting of their sins. Immediately they were filled with the Holy Spirit as in Acts chapter 2: they began to speak out with messages in tongues, and others interpreted.

As these mullahs heard of each other's experiences, they were thirsty to learn more about Jesus. Subsequently, they sent two representatives to the capital city of Sofia to seek help and advice. On the streets, these two mullahs began to ask, "What kind of people worship Jesus and speak in unknown languages with interpretations and have people healed in their services?"

Somebody suggested that they visit the Bulgarian Pentecostal Church, where they were introduced to an evangelist to the Balkan States from the Assemblies of God, who documented this story.

In the gripping book *The Torn Veil*, Pakistani former cripple Gulshan Esther recounts her wonderful testimony; she heard the voice of Jesus quoting the Muslim holy book—the section about Jesus the

Healer. All medical help failed her in her quest to be healed. Later Jesus appeared to her with the 12 apostles and totally healed her! She was also given supernatural instructions to find a Holy Bible.

George Otis Jr., in *The Last of the Giants*, outlines accounts from the early 1980s of supernatural conversions falling into three basic categories: through dreams and visitations, through miraculous healings, and through special deliverances (both physical and spiritual).

Otis reports that the magnitude of these phenomena is so great that some missionary organizations are taking the time to reexamine doctrinal positions relative to issues such as divine healing. He wrote:

> In the early 1980s a truly remarkable incident took place in a North African village located 125 miles east of Algiers. According to testimony, on one unforgettable night in 1983, with no prior warning and for no immediately discernible reason—God sovereignly descended upon this coastal township. Moving from house to house, and communicating through a combination of dreams, visions and angelic visitations, He did not rest until every member of this Muslim community was properly introduced to His only begotten Son, Jesus. Come daybreak, nearly every villager had a story to tell. A sense of spiritual awe settled over the entire village. In the weeks that followed, their conclusions led to a dramatic wholesale conversion involving from 400 to 450 Muslim villagers—that was a nearly eighteen-fold increase in the size of the entire Algerian national church!

> When amazed mission workers, who had had no direct involvement in this extraordinary development, began to investigate possible reasons for this sovereign visitation, they came across a stunning piece of information. It was at virtually this very site that in 1315 a Spanish missionary named Raymond Lull had been stoned to death by Muslims after he preached in the open market. It has often been said that the blood of the martyrs is the seed of the church. Lull is generally considered to be the first missionary to Muslims.

God will also communicate in dreams and visions to empower us for service, especially for very arduous service. An account from the IsaalMasih.net ("Jesus Is Messiah") Web site is a case in point:

> A North Africa believer in Jesus found the needed strength to face his imprisonment from a dream he experienced while imprisoned for his faith. In the dream, he saw thousands of believers pouring through the streets of his city, openly proclaiming their faith in his restricted country. While in prison, he was tortured, suspended upside-down for hours, beaten with electrified rods and repeatedly threatened with execution. His vision of a day when people of his country would openly proclaim their faith in the streets gave him great strength to persevere through this most difficult time in his life.

ASK, SEEK, KNOCK

"And ye shall seek Me, and find Me, when ye shall search for Me with all your heart. And I will be found of you, saith the Lord: and I will turn away your captivity, and I will gather you from all the nations, and from all the places whither I have driven you, saith the Lord; and I will bring you again into the place whence I caused you to be carried away captive," the Almighty promises in the Bible in Jeremiah 29:13-14.

Many of the divine dreams contain clues, which are meant to cause a hunger for Jesus and to trigger the process of seeking Him.

During the Muslim fasting month of Ramadan, a young Muslim from the Indonesian island of Kalimantan (formerly Borneo) experienced a disturbing dream: he was tied to a chair with heavy, thick ropes. A man he recognized as Jesus touched the ropes, and they fell from his arms. Jesus then said to him, "Look for the pole."

"What pole?" he asked, but Jesus simply reiterated, "Look for the pole."

The young man awakened from his dream pondering the meaning of the pole, but in a few days he forgot about the dream because of the daily cares of life. But two years later, again during the Muslim fasting month of Ramadan, another dream occurred. This time Jesus visited the young man saying, "Why haven't you done what I asked? I told you to look for the pole."

"Where is this pole and how can I find it?" the young man asked, perplexed.

Jesus pointed to a hill very far away and said, "Go look for the pole."

In his dream, the man ran in the direction in which Jesus had pointed. He seemed to run for miles through thorns and dense undergrowth, and finally, exhausted, he came to a clearing. To his utter surprise, before him stood the Cross! This was the pole the Lord Jesus had told him to find.

The next day, the young man visited his mosque and asked the leader if he knew the meaning of the dreams and the Cross. The imam wisely replied, "Search for the truth."

"Is the Christian Jesus the truth then?"

But the imam just repeated, "Search for the truth."

The next night the young man dreamed again, and this time he saw a cemetery. He recognized the graves as Christian—all were decorated with crosses. Suddenly, the graves were opened! Those who were buried rose into the sky, where Jesus was waiting for them. He cried out to Jesus that he wasn't ready because he did not yet have the Cross.

Awakening from this dream, the young man was greatly distressed. He knew of a small church near his village, so he visited the church to seek help from the pastor, who gave him a Bible. They opened the pages to John 14:6, "Jesus saith unto him, 'I am the way, the truth, and the life.'"

THE SIGN OF THE CROSS

One of the most remarkable testimonies concerning dreams and visions in the Middle East involves a very brave brother, whom I'll call Issa, from the Orthodox Church. Many years ago, when my husband and I lived in a suburb of Jerusalem, we held Christmas parties and house meetings where the power of God was manifested mightily with

Jewish and Arab friends in attendance. One of the young men who received a saving knowledge of the Lord was Issa. He has stood faithfully in his hometown and has grown tremendously in the Lord. He was also one of the first persons to host an evangelistic meeting for our ministry in the Middle East, so he is doubly precious to me.

Within recent years, Issa has received several dramatic visitations from the Lord, who instructed him to construct large crosses to change the skyline of his city. Because of his obedience to the heavenly vision, the skyline has indeed changed dramatically, especially at nighttime, with an abundance of large, bright white and red crosses atop buildings and hotels. Although demographically his city used to be a Christian town, most of the Christians have left through intimidation from Islam, and now most of the residents are Muslims. Issa is a simple street vendor; yet he is the kind of humble person whom the Lord often calls.

The first time the Lord instructed Issa in a night vision to erect crosses in the Holy Land, Jesus said, "Issa, Issa, trouble is coming, but you will raise up the sign of the Cross just as Moses lifted up the snake on the pole in the wilderness. And when the people look to the Cross, as they looked at the snake on the pole in the wilderness, they will live because of the Cross."

Issa emphasized to me, "The Lord said when the people look to the Cross, they will believe and live."

I personally know this to be true. An Arab named Mohammed who secretly loved the Lord and who prayed the sinner's prayer with me was once traveling through an Israeli checkpoint without proper papers. He was in peril of being jailed. But when he looked at one of the illuminated crosses, Mohammed took fresh courage, and he managed to evade danger by obtaining favor at the checkpoint.

At first, Issa was timid and reluctant, so he fashioned only one simple cross to display in his city. He thought that by that one act he had obeyed the Lord. But Jesus appeared to him a second time and told him not to stop displaying the crosses. There are now more than 18 of these large crosses that Issa has erected.

The Lord admonished him this time, "Issa! Issa! Just as I told the Israelites to put the Blood of the Lamb over the doorposts and they lived because of the protection of that blood, so I command you to raise up the Cross in the Middle East, and people will look and live." Pray for the continuing protection and boldness of this unusually brave man.

THE SIGN OF THE COMMUNION CUP

"Young men shall see visions." The Holy Spirit's saga in the Bible lands continues. While ministering in the church in Kuwait, I met a wonderful young man, whom I'll call Ahmed from Saudi Arabia. Because he had studied to be a leader in his regional mosque, and because of being a Saudi national, Ahmed had no knowledge whatsoever of the Christian church. Yet one day, without any prior knowledge of Christ, Ahmed experienced a remarkable vision.

Ahmed saw a large church descending from heaven. Inside the edifice he heard people singing the most beautiful and glorious music he had ever heard. In fact, he had never heard any music like it on earth before, nor has he heard it since. (Worshippers don't sing hymns and choruses in mosques.) He saw people from every nation in this building worshipping and praising the living God. Down the center aisle swiftly approaching him was a majestic man, who extended to Ahmed a silver cup. The Man said to him, "From the moment you drink from this cup you are mine."

Determined to understand this mysterious but glorious vision, Ahmed visited Kuwait, a neighboring Arab country, where church buildings on a compound are permitted, unlike in Saudi Arabia. The first church he visited belonged to the Roman Catholics. He entered while a Mass was being conducted, and he received the communion, but he did not fully know what he was doing. Afterward, the priest suggested that Ahmed should visit the nearby Orthodox Church, where he saw an icon of Christ. This was the man of the vision! The

Orthodox priest suggested that Ahmed should visit the nearby Evangelical Church, where he was extended the right hand of fellowship.

Remarkably, other Arabs are receiving visions and strength from the cup of Christ! Khalid in Jerusalem told us his remarkable story on a visit to his humble home in East Jerusalem:

"As you know," Khalid began, "I've been a believer in Jesus for several years because of dreams and visions. I even began to evangelize and lead other Arabs to the Lord. But I did not realize what a clever enemy new believers have in satan, who does not want anybody to come to the knowledge of the truth. So for several years the devil managed to lure me back onto drugs, and I was a heroin addict. My wife and my children and all my family despised me because I could not kick the habit, no matter how many times I was in the hospital for rehabilitation. I tried to kill myself, but even failed at that.

"Finally, I said to the Lord, 'I am going home and I will trust you and you only to deliver me, as the drugs in the hospital that are supposed to cure me are making me crave heroin more!' So I came home trusting Jesus and Jesus alone. He appeared to me in a vision. I could see Him as clearly as I see you now. He was holding in His hands a big silver cup, and He told me to drink from it. But when I looked inside, I was afraid, because it was full of blood [representative of the atoning blood of Jesus Christ]. But He told me not to be afraid and to drink. He said, 'Drink from the cup of salvation.' When I tasted it, it did not taste like blood, but it was sweet to taste like a heavenly wine, and instantly all the desire for heroin disappeared from me!

"But," Khalid continued, "although I knew I was now set free, I also knew I was a swept clean and empty house that satan could overpower again if I was not careful, which is what happened before. So this time the Lord came to me again in a vision. I saw Him motioning for me to follow Him into the desert, the place where He went when He endured a forty-day fast to overcome the devil. I am going to take only a donkey, a tent, and a water supply, and I am going to follow that vision and go into the desert and fast for forty days to get the power over drugs and the powers of darkness that are trying to destroy my life and my witness."

We prayed with much might for Khalid to be strengthened. I told him, "Remember that the angels came and ministered to Jesus while He was fasting in the wilderness and overcoming satan by the Word of God, so if you feel faint or desperate or tempted, call on the Lord, and I know He will send His angels to help you."

Although at the time Khalid was very thin, he reported later that he had survived the fast. When he felt the weakest, he said he could hear believers praying for him, and he overcame by the blood of the Lamb and the word of his testimony!

DREAM CONCERNING SADDAM HUSSEIN

In a dream in 2005, I was on a bus with Saddam Hussein, who was thin, haggard, and dressed in a dirty white robe. He was being transported as a captive of the U.S. government, and it was my responsibility to watch him. But he didn't want to escape! He wanted to be comforted for his sins. In the dream, he prayed the sinner's prayer and I told him, "What would it have profited you, if you had gained the whole world and yet lost your soul?" He agreed. He soundly repented for all of his evil deeds and received Jesus—yes, even this mass murderer and cruel tyrant was repentant, and asked Jesus into his heart in this vivid dream. Then he leaned on my shoulder and wept.

Just as Saddam's cruel mentor, Nebuchadnezzar, was debased, crawled in the dirt like an animal for seven years, and eventually acknowledged the God of Israel, so Saddam was debased and was captured from a hole in the ground. It is not impossible for any Islamic leader to receive revelation of Jesus! When our team visited Baghdad in 2002, six months prior to the U.S. invasion, the Lord led us during a communion service to remit the sins of Saddam (John 20:23), just as Jesus had earlier led us to remit the sins of Jordan's King Hussein on the day he passed away.

An intercessor who receives many pictures from the Lord sent me a drawing of Iran's troublesome leader bowing down to his god in the palm of a gigantic hand, but the hand was lifeless stone. She wrote to me, "He is sincere, but sincerely wrong." Muslim leaders are religiously and sincerely zealous but lack revelation as to who the real God is. If believers will pray fervently—as we have been supplicating for nearly two decades in Jerusalem—that the Islamic leaders will experience dreams and visions of Jesus, the world will experience a mighty revival.

ENDNOTES

1. Edward Rice, *Captain Sir Richard Francis Burton* (New York: Scribner's, 1990).

2. Tarif Khalidi, *The Muslim Jesus: Sayings and Stories in Islamic Literature* (Cambridge, MA: Harvard University Press, 2001).

3. A mullah is a respected teacher in a mosque.

CHAPTER 4

Multitudes Reaching for Jesus

More than two hundred million people live in the cauldron of the Middle East. Imagine the scene of such masses clutching at the hem of Jesus' robes!

A vision granted to an Arab who lives near the Temple Mount (the *Haram Al Sharif*) in Jerusalem depicted Jesus as our "great high priest, that is passed into the heavens" (Hebrews 4:14), making intercession for "multitudes in the valley of decision" (Joel 3:14). What is especially interesting is that this vision was seen by a former Muslim who lives in Jerusalem.

"I saw Jesus dressed as the high priest in the Temple and His hair was as white as snow and His eyes were flaming like fire," he said. The vision of this born-again believer in Jesus as Lord was similar to John's description of Jesus' physical features in the first chapter of the Book of Revelation. "I also saw the wounds in his hands and the glory shining from his face filled the sky like lightning."

The Holy Spirit is outpouring revelation in great magnitude in the Middle East through the divine agencies of dreams and visions in fulfillment of Joel 2:28: "Your old men shall dream dreams, your young men shall see visions."

Multitudes of Middle Easterners in the Valley of Decision are reaching by faith for Jesus in the secret counsels of their hearts. Many tell me furtively in person, or via the Internet, that they already believe in Him, but except for fear of rejection and retaliation from their families and peers, they would be more open about Jesus.

The day will come when the name of Jesus will be upon the lips of multitudes in the Middle East who will no longer keep silent but will realize that they are part of the end-time mass movement of the Holy Spirit.

The spirit of revelation has increased greatly upon both Jew and Arab, especially since our many prophetic conferences in the Holy Land, where we encourage God's people to believe that the spirit of grace and supplications will be outpoured as prophesied in Zechariah 12:10:

> *And I will pour upon the house of David, and upon the inhabitants of Jerusalem, the Spirit of grace and of supplications: and they shall look upon Me whom they have pierced, and they shall mourn for Him, as one mourneth for his only son, and shall be in bitterness for Him, as one that is in bitterness for his firstborn.*

NEW REVIVAL IN OLD CITY OF JERUSALEM

Since the Day of Pentecost, prayer has preceded every awakening. After more than a decade of intensive Spirit-led corporate intercessory prayer in Jerusalem for the release of the captives in the Middle East, we began to see more dramatic answers. The strong man is bound when we pray corporately (Mark 3:27). The god of this age has blinded the captives to the light of the glorious Gospel (2 Corinthians 4:4).

But satan's grip is becoming arthritic as we loose captives and execute the judgments written against him in the Word of God (Psalm 149). And as we worship and praise the Lord, the Holy Spirit continues to outpour the spirit of revelation (Joel 2:28).

In Jerusalem's Old City, we personally know many believers who confess a saving knowledge of the Lord through the divine agencies of dreams and visions. These believers, many of whom are former drug addicts, pray together regularly. They also sponsor bold evangelistic outreaches. We continue to pray that God will raise up a strong five-fold ministry, especially pastors with a shepherd's heart, in the Bible Lands. One of the strongest of these leaders is Pastor Samir, our beloved translator in our own bold evangelistic outreaches inside the Old City Walls at "The Fountain."

Zechariah is another believer in the current Revival. One day he visited the Church of the Holy Sepulcher in the Old City. He put his hand on the empty tomb and prayed to the Lord, "In the same way You shook the world when You were resurrected, I want this power in my life!" Zechariah threw away his pills and hashish. Resisting the cravings, he attended a prayer conference, but he could not concentrate on the messages. He decided to go to bed with the Bible in his hands. He began to read the Psalms and then fell into a deep sleep. He dreamt he was in a dark prison, with a window the size of his mouth. He put his lips around the small prison aperture and began calling upon the name of Jesus in desperation. Jesus' shadow was strong enough to break the prison locks! As the door swung open, Zechariah beheld the glory of God more dazzling than any light imaginable. Jesus gave him a golden ring. Zechariah awakened and was instantly delivered. He has progressed with the Lord after a number of years and trials.

Ibrihim and his brother also related their revelations and interpretations while drinking tea in a little falafel restaurant run by Pastor Samir. I call it the "Falafel Chapel" because videos and testimonies of Jesus are always playing for the customers. Many divine appointments take place in this humble little snack bar. Just the night before, Ibrihim's brother had dreamed that a dead friend sent a message from hell. Consequently, he was deeply convicted to rescue others from hell's horrors.

Ibrihim recalled his own startling vision of Jesus standing above the Dome of the Rock shrine at the Temple Mount (*Haram Al Sharif*). Jesus was knocking on the door of every mosque, every synagogue, and every home in Jerusalem! Ibrihim said, "God is visiting this city again—and every house and every person and every corner will hear the Gospel of Jesus Christ, whether they are Jews, Muslims, Armenians or whatever. It is the time of visitation. There is a tremendous hunger and thirst that I have never seen here before."

A former Muslim, Evangelist Dahood at first fluctuated about his commitment to Christ. Religious spirits clouded and tormented his mind. But Jesus began to reveal Himself through dreams, visions, and Bible study. In the past he has been beaten, stripped, and tortured by fanatics who demanded that he stop preaching. Dahood answers, his face shining like an angel, "Praise Jesus! You may kill my body, but you cannot destroy my soul."

Rabbi Yeshua (Hebrew for Jesus), runs a synagogue in the Old City. Like many Jewish people in the current stage of their soon-coming awakening, he is very open. During our divine encounter, Rabbi Yeshua admitted his fascination with *the* Rabbi Yeshua. Many Jewish people over the world are seeing visions of Jesus, and to their great surprise, many of them discover that He is Jewish, the Son of David!

MANY WILL BE RAPTURED OUT OF ISRAEL

Matthew Schwartz, a Messianic Jewish leader, led a group of tourists to Israel because he had a burden to pray. Speaking at The Cornerstone World Outreach Center in Springfield, Missouri, he spoke about an amazing experience that happened while his group visited Tel Aviv.

Matthew and his group were marching down the streets of Tel Aviv in parade-like fashion. They were singing choruses and encouraging people.

While the group was passing a store, the owner of the store, a 72-year-old Jewish man named Moshe came out to talk to them. He told this amazing story:

> My wife and I moved here to Israel years ago because we wanted to be here when the Messiah came. We are waiting for His coming.
>
> I have been having a recurring dream the last three months, and it is disturbing me, because I keep having this same

dream over and over again. I have been to the Rabbis; I have talked to four or five of them, and none of them can interpret my dream.

Then he said, "Can you help me? Can you explain it to me and tell me what it means?"

Pastor Lane, who was a part of the group answered him, "I don't know if I can, but let me hear your dream."

He called Matthew over and five or six others joined them, to listen to the story about the old man's dream.

> I keep dreaming that I am awakened up from sleep, in my bed, in the middle of the night. I dream that trumpets are sounding, and I run to the front door and look out, and thousands of people from the nation of Israel are going up through the clouds, and they are wearing white robes, and the heavens are parting, and the angel Gabriel is standing in the heavens, blowing a trumpet. And there is a rider on a white horse, with thousands of armies behind him. The man on the horse is "The Conqueror." I have had this dream about twenty times in the last ninety days. I told my wife. I say, "I see a man on a white horse."

He had never read the New Testament. But he knew the Old Testament, and he knew that there are two archangels. He knew that one is the angel Gabriel.

He said, "No one understands it. I told my wife, the rabbis, and the people in the store, but no one can interpret it."

Pastor Lane Matthew, and the others opened the New Testament and read to him from 1 Thessalonians, chapter 4:

> *For this we say unto you by the word of the Lord, that we which are alive and remain unto the coming of the Lord shall not prevent them which are asleep. For the Lord Himself shall descend from Heaven with a shout, with the voice of the archangel, and with the trump of God: and the dead in Christ shall rise first:*

then we which are alive and remain shall be caught up together with them in the clouds, to meet the Lord in the air: and so shall we ever be with the Lord.

When the old man heard it, he exclaimed excitedly, "That is my dream!"

When they explained that The Conqueror was Yeshua, his Messiah, he began to cry.

So they asked, "Do you want to ask Jesus Christ into your life?"

He said, "Yes." And he was born again, right there on Diezengoff Street in Tel Aviv!

SHI'ITE MUSLIM ALSO DREAMS ABOUT THE RAPTURE

My friend Jim Bramlett, an author and faithful watchman for the Second Coming of Jesus, sent me the following testimony, which he verified by telephone:

Ali, a former Shi'ite Muslim from Iran, was shaken by a supernatural experience. He was living on the West Coast of the United States. Ali experienced a night vision during which Jesus spoke to him, and he subsequently became a Spirit-filled believer.

A few months later, Ali experienced another vivid night vision, this time concerning the pre-tribulation Rapture, the awesome future event when the Lord will appear in the clouds to remove all believers who are watching for His return. Ali had never studied the doctrine of the Second Coming. He had also never heard of the Rapture, the soon-coming event described by the Apostle Paul in 1 Thessalonians 4:16-17:

For the Lord himself shall descend from Heaven with a shout, with the voice of the archangel, and with the trump of God: and the dead in Christ shall rise first: then we which are alive and remain shall be caught up [= raptured, a word derived from the Latin Vulgate version of the Bible] *together with them in the clouds, to meet the Lord in the air: and so shall we ever be with the Lord.*

Ali envisioned the Rapture in the night vision without any prior theological knowledge of the "catching away" of believers by Jesus into the clouds. Ali also claims that the Lord revealed to him the city where he will reside when the Rapture occurs. In the second dream, Ali was raptured from a certain Midwestern city of the United States. His Muslim uncle was left behind in tears, because the uncle suddenly realized that everything Ali had shared about Jesus was true, and the Tribulation Period was therefore about to start.

Ali waited, not understanding how everything will come to pass. But two years later, he surprisingly received a telephone call from this uncle, who asked him to move to the Midwestern city of the Rapture dream. Ali now manages his uncle's shop and resides in the city from where he was snatched to heaven in the dream.

Ali therefore believes the Rapture is imminent, although he will not speculate exactly when. He is saddened that few pastors teach about the Rapture and the Second Coming of Jesus.

Ali's story is another "wake-up call" that Jesus is coming soon. How fascinating that the preacher is a former Shi'ite Muslim and not an American TV evangelist!

GREAT MOVE OF GOD IN JERICHO

A significant work of God in the Middle East began at the Jesus House of Prayer in Jericho. It was led by my friend Pastor Terry Mac-Intosh and his volunteers. I have been privileged on several occasions to preach and to minister in the Jesus House of Prayer, and it was this organization that backed our ministry's daring seven-day Jericho March and evangelistic outreach in Jericho. We believed that God would set all of the captives free in the Middle East!

In fact, our Jericho March in Jericho was a prophetic parable to believe that God would make all of the walls in the Middle East collapse. We were like the "battering ram of the Holy Ghost." After our team conducted the seven-day march, according to the Biblical pattern, a few Muslims who were wanting to stone us threw down their stones and began to praise the Lord at the sound of the *victory shout!* This was a perfect example and harbinger of the power of spiritual warfare to set the captives free.

That night a door opened for me to preach with a full sound system in Jericho's city square. Pastor Terry arranged this daring meeting. Even though Hamas terrorists opposed the event over mosque loud-speakers, Palestinian authorities restrained them and police protected our team with their armed presence. One hundred and forty-four seekers received copies of the *Jesus* film after the event that night in the open square as team members ministered to Palestinians.

The Jesus House of Prayer also helped us to conduct one of our evangelistic outreaches in a large Bedouin tent restaurant in the Jericho City of Palms. Pastor Terry also organized a March for Jesus in Jericho—truly a "first!"— with a parade and banners. Terry recorded the outpouring of dreams and visions among the seekers and believers. One of the reports was headlined:

Jesus Appears in Jericho

One of our young men friends has believed upon Jesus and followed through with all the external motions as evidence of his faith. Lately, however, he has been bombarded with negative influences all around him. His father requires him to read the Koran every day and to attend certain meetings on a regular basis. He has also found himself involved with dangerous characters who have certain expectations of him. Because of all the brainwashing, he came to a point of questioning his salvation and asking if all this about Jesus is real. To top it all off, he was in an accident a few nights ago.

Later, in confusion and perplexity, our friend went to the roof, thinking to sleep there. He began to pray with a sincere heart, and he asked God who He really is, and what the real truth is. According to him, a bright light appeared before him, and a voice spoke to him out of it. It said, "Follow Me."

The light then sped up and away out of sight. That was a close encounter that happened quickly, but it was enough to convince him that Jesus is the Way! He says he was not asleep, and that it was a wide-awake experience. He did not know what to do, so he just praised God for a long time.

Today, he knows it was Jesus who came to him. Jesus is alive! He is greatly encouraged, just as he should be!

Another testimony just today came from a Palestinian woman who claims that Jesus visited her in a dream. He was dressed in silver, and the whole scene was saturated in the same color. He was wearing a cross in her dream.

Jesus disappeared, but suddenly in her vision, she appeared to be wearing the exact same kind of clothing as Jesus! We were able to help her to see that since she is clothed by faith in Christ, she is becoming more like him. She, too, is encouraged.

Karen Dunham is another daring woman who subsequently has moved into Jericho. She is reaping from the groundwork that Pastor Terry, others, and we have faithfully laid in the ancient City of the Palms. One plants, another waters, but it is God who gives the increase. Karen is feeding the poor, as is the Jesus House of Prayer. She told me about a man named Mohammed who had seen a vision of Jesus sitting with scissors at a table. Jesus was cutting designs out of folded paper. When Jesus opened the paper, it was cut in the shape of a Cross and Arabic words warning about hell!

THE DARK SPEECH OF GOD

The reader may ask, why does God speak in riddles and in enigmas that are not always easy to fathom and to understand?

"I will open my mouth in a parable: I will utter dark sayings of old" (Psalm 78:2) is a verse that describes the "dark speech" of God. *Dark speech* is speech consisting of riddles and pictures that the Lord often employs when communicating with us. The old adage "a picture is worth a thousand words" is certainly true of the economical way in which God often speaks to us.

Furthermore, the Hebrew word in the Bible translated "dark speech" or "dark saying" is *chidah*, which literally means "a knot." Often we have to unravel what God is saying to us. It is part of the seeking process that indicates sincerity of heart. But one word from God can release a life-changing blessing, as we see in the lives of the persons in this book.

One dream or vision from God can be brief, but it can also result in a far-reaching encounter and can instantly impart fresh direction.

Many times God has spoken to me with clear and very simple commands. Often I have seen Him in a vision leading me to a certain place; in such a vision, the Lord may look back at me questioningly, as if to say, "Are you going to follow Me?" Or He will speak in a dream and simply tell me to go somewhere. That is very plain guidance. But other dreams, visions, and communications from God are more complicated in their outworking, causing us to seek His face with all of our hearts.

Sometimes in our lives God shows us the big headlines, but the fine print needs to be discerned and worked out day by day. If we could always be sure of hearing from God perfectly and accurately, our tendency, unfortunately, would be to become prideful and puffed up. Therefore, God also employs the dark speech of dreams and visions to keep us humble and seeking him for fresh revelation. He is always looking for a faith response from us. As one Christian leader has said, "Nobody graduates in the School of Listening or from the School of Spiritual Guidance with his pride intact."

In Mark 4:33-34 we are told, "And with many such parables spake He the word unto them, as they were able to hear it. But without a parable spake He not unto them: and when they were alone, He expounded all things to His disciples."

So from time to time God varies his many ways of communicating to keep us on our spiritual toes. Dark speech certainly does develop a dependency in our lives to seek the Lord step by step.

Dark speech is an indirect way in which God speaks. Sometimes we may assume God is saying one thing only to discover later that He was actually indicating something quite different. This does not mean that God is capricious. He just requires us to unravel the message by praying and seeking His face earnestly. According to 1 Corinthians

13:9-12 (NKJV), "For now we see in a mirror, dimly, but then face to face." The word "dimly" literally means "in a riddle," or "in an enigma." Also in Numbers 12:8, the Lord reveals one of His "m.o.'s" (methods of communication), "With him will I speak mouth to mouth, even apparently, and not in dark speeches [riddles]."

MOROCCAN LAMB

Reports of revelations in the Muslim world sometimes involve not only dreams and visions but also miracles of confirmation that the Bible is indeed true. A case in point is from Morocco.

Rachid, a young Muslim, watched "by chance" a TV broadcast of the *Jesus* film. He was deeply moved by the Gospel story and responded to an address on the TV screen to request a Bible. He received an Arabic *Injil*, the New Testament.

As Rachid began to read for himself the story he had experienced in the film, he literally fell in love with the Word. He reveled in Christ's love and His many miracles and took Jesus to his heart. He was a Moroccan lamb who was seeking the Good Shepherd. Still, as a practicing Muslim, Rachid continued to attend Friday service at his local mosque. The religious leader, however, strongly warned his congregation against watching the *Jesus* film and requesting Bibles.

Rachid could not bring himself to forfeit his New Testament. He continued to read it at night until he fell asleep. Then one night, Jesus appeared to him, clothed in a beautiful white robe. Calling him by name, Jesus said, "Rachid, you are going to be one of My children. You will be a child of God."

Rachid awoke and was troubled, because he did not fully understand the theological message of Jesus in the dream. He decided to go to his mosque to seek answers. He dared to share his dream with the religious leader, adding: "Sir, I am really sorry I disobeyed your orders, but can you tell me what my dream means?"

The leader of the mosque replied threateningly, "Oh, Rachid, you are evil. I warned you! Now go home and burn this book, or you will indeed burn in hell! You must do as I tell you immediately!"

Sorrowfully but obediently, the Moroccan returned home and started a fire. He threw his beloved New Testament into the flames. It was such a personal loss that he could not watch the desecration. With tears in his eyes, he left his house to take a long walk.

When Rachid returned home, he sorrowfully sifted through the ashes. The *Injil* was destroyed, yet he was fascinated to find the remains of one verse! He picked up the scrap and blew off the ashes. Amazingly, a personal message from John 1:12 had been preserved: "But as many as received Him, to them gave He power to become the sons of God." This was a Biblical allusion to the actual message Jesus had spoken to him in the dream! — "Rachid, you are going to be one of My children. You will be a child of God."

Rachid sent a letter to the director of the *Jesus* Film Project for the Middle East, saying, "I knew then that I *could* be a child of God because that was the only verse in the Bible that did not burn.... I now know I shall not burn in hell, but will live with Jesus forever!"

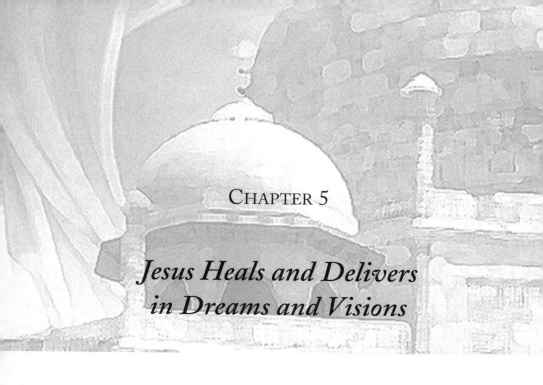

CHAPTER 5

Jesus Heals and Delivers in Dreams and Visions

The incidents in this chapter are some of the most dramatic healing miracles of our day. I have personally met and interviewed the Arab woman in the following account and she has testified in one of our public services.

Not far from our former ministry center on the Mount of Olives, a Muslim woman experienced a remarkable vision. Jesus visited her in a night vision and said in Arabic, "I am the Lord; put your trust in no prophet. Follow me." Fatima was afraid and chose not to believe. She rolled over in her bed and pretended the whole experience had not happened.

But the following day, while cooking at her tiny stove, Fatima spilled hot oil down her leg. The burn was so severe that her flesh melted. She was rushed to the hospital, and her leg was heavily bandaged.

That night in a dream, the Lord Jesus visited Fatima a second time.

"You did not believe Me before," He said, "but to prove to you that I AM, your leg shall be healed."

In the morning, when Fatima swung her legs out of the bed, suddenly she noticed that her injured limb was pain free and totally healed. The skin was as new and supple as a baby's.

Though she searched diligently through her bedclothes and everywhere in her house, she could not find any trace of the bandages! The Lord's goodness and hand have blessed Fatima, her husband, and their children with salvation. Her testimony has been shared far and wide, and much glory has been attributed to the Risen Savior!

MUNZER'S DREAM: JESUS VISITS ANOTHER MOSQUE

Munzer is one of my great friends in Jerusalem. He comes from an aristocratic Arab family and has been extremely helpful to our ministry by supplying Middle Eastern–styled Gospel tents.

Many years ago, I led Munzer in a sinner's prayer. I (and my prayer partner Miri) had visited him in his shop at a point when he was going to hang himself because he was desperately in debt. Immediately Miri began to pray in tongues while I shared the Good News with Munzer. He received Jesus and was greatly helped by the Lord. But Munzer had not grown much in the Lord because of Muslim family ties.

However, Mohammed, one of Munzer's sons, with his father's permission, had also become a believer and had changed his name in order to move more freely in the Messianic community. Meanwhile, Munzer's health was never good.

One day I saw Munzer and immediately exclaimed, "What has happened to you?" He looked radiant. Light was streaming from his face. He looked almost as young as his son and he appeared extremely healthy and full of vitality!

"Christine, I *must* tell you what happened!" Munzer enthused.

"Ten days ago, I had a dream. I was in a mosque with my son Mohammed, and we were praying together. Jesus walked into the mosque where we were praying, and the floor was changed into the most dazzling layers of gemstones that you can imagine—more beautiful than I have ever seen on earth! He was dressed in white and his face shone like the moon. He put his hands on our heads and blessed us. I felt like in the dream that He had put his hand on my head for at least five minutes. I feel so much better, and I know I am healed."

I took great delight in rejoicing with my brother Munzer and reading to him Revelation 21:19-21. Those verses describe in great detail the priceless gemstones in the foundations of Heaven. Truly Munzer's dream had been heavenly.

Some readers may have a problem with Jesus blessing somebody in a mosque. But I always say that Jesus continues to walk through walls to seek the lost sheep of the House of Islam.

SUPERNATURAL IS THE KEY

The Christian Broadcasting Network (CBN) in recent years has been producing awesome documentaries in both the Arabic and Hausa languages concerning persons who have been healed through dreams and visions. In the video *Muzika*, produced by Victor Oladokun in Nigeria, the real life testimony of Mohammed Ali is dramatically portrayed.

Inside Mohammed Ali there was a vacuum. He sat down one day to think deeply about his life and problems. He turned to God and prayed. From that day onward, his life would never be the same.

"God held me with his right hand," Mohammed Ali continued, "and lifted me high to where the angels are. An angel came to me with a very black man. The man was handcuffed. His feet were tied. He was dripping with blood all over his body. I was told that the man was an adulterer, a liar, and one who makes a bribe. He was involved in every kind of evil. It was said that before God this man stood already condemned. I was asked what I thought about the man. I asked if he was really a human being. On taking a good look at him, you could see a life battered by sin. However, I said to the angels that if he was a man, he should be forgiven his sins. I said that even though his sins were many, he stood before a loving God. Because of God's mercy he should be forgiven. The angels turned to me and said that this pitiful man was none other than myself!"

Mohammed Ali was granted several other similar experiences. From his childhood, his parents cherished the hope that he would become an Islamic teacher.

"In spite of achieving a position in my community as a teacher, I was not a happy man inside. I was scared of what will happen to me on Judgment Day. I was constantly bothered by a question: where will I go after death—Heaven or hell? I continued to search for the way of salvation. It was this search that led to my changed life."

One night about ten years ago, Mohammed Ali was meditating on his bed when suddenly, "I saw the Heaven open. I heard voices. Then Jesus Himself appeared to me! With a calm and soothing voice, He said, 'I will help you.' But I thought He had come to make me rich. I thought that meeting Him would be the solution to my poverty."

The Risen Jesus Christ continued to reveal Himself to Mohammed Ali through dreams and various visions, yet his life did not alter, because he was resisting Jesus. He did not submit his life to the Lord's will.

Although Mohammed Ali was married, he committed adultery with a neighbor. On his way home, he was met by a total stranger who asked him piercingly, "Where have you come from?" Mohammed Ali was angry at the question. But then something fearful happened. The stranger suddenly vanished before his eyes! Mohammed Ali was quite frightened. He ran home. As soon as he reached home, he said his prayers. He asked for God's help and forgiveness.

Not long after, Mohammed Ali experienced yet another encounter:

"While I was asleep I heard a knock on my door. I woke up and opened the door. I asked who was out there. I told whoever was knocking at the door to come in. There was no one at the door. I went back to sleep.

"After a short while I heard a voice saying, 'Mohammed Ali, come to me. I am Jesus Christ.' I opened my eyes and, behold, Jesus stood before me! He shone with dazzling brightness. He kept calling me to come to Him. His voice was very sweet. I cannot compare it to anything I've ever heard on earth."

One day, Mohammed Ali went to visit a friend. On his way he met Pastor Emmanuel Kyari. He told the Pastor the story of his encounters with Jesus. The pastor took Mohammed Ali home and explained the humanity of Jesus Christ from the Scriptures. He showed him the way of salvation through Jesus Christ.

What a joy! Mohammed Ali came to the end of his search. Pastor Kyari recited John 14:6: "Jesus saith unto him, I am the way, the truth, and the life: no man cometh unto the Father, but by Me."

On hearing God's Word, Mohammed Ali testified, "I have seen God's mercies in the life of a sinner like me. The Lord is gracious. He forgave my sins. I now know that even though I die I will live again. That is the assurance I have in Christ Jesus."

Mohammed Ali invited Jesus into his life as his Savior. What followed? Persecutions! His wife divorced him. His parents forsook him. His house was set ablaze. Yet Mohammed Ali said, "I am not ashamed of the name of Jesus Christ wherever I go."

Today, Mohammed Ali's life is completely changed. He has new life in Christ and is preaching the glorious Gospel.

Secularly speaking, Mohammed Ali's lifestyle is worse since he became a Christian. He's lost his wife, his house, and all his belongings, and he is cut off from his parents. However, he affirms,

"In God's love and mercy, he has replaced all that I've lost. He has given me brothers and sisters in Christ, food, and clothing.

"The Lord has shown me great love. His grace saw me through the trying period. He has kept and preserved me till this day. He is a loving God. He is worthy of all praise and worship. Even if no one else praises the Lord, I have every reason to praise Him for His goodness in my life."

WITH GOD NOTHING IS IMPOSSIBLE:
SHEIK HEALED OF AIDS

On the other side of Africa in the East, in Ethiopia, CBN TV cameras have documented another spectacular miracle. A man was healed of AIDS through a Jesus vision, and there is hospital documentation to prove it.

Sheik Mohamid Amin was born in the Juna Province of Ethiopia to the son of a goatherd and a mother who was barren for many years. Like Hannah, the mother of Samuel the Bible prophet, Mohamid's mother was so desperate for children that she made a vow to God. If God would grant her a son, her child would become the servant of the Lord all his days.

From his childhood, Mohamid studied the Koran; later he was sent to Oman to study, where he won a scholarship to Saudi Arabia. While he was in Arabia, he prayed fervently and awakened at 2 A.M. to begin his prayers.

"My dream was to spread Islam in Ethiopia and in the world. But one thing constantly troubled me. Something was missing. I could find no inner peace, no matter how long I prayed or studied."

Nine years later, Mohamid returned to his native Ethiopia and earned a position in one of the largest mosques. He left to study in the Sudan, and when he returned to Ethiopia at age 30, his health was rapidly failing.

> "I was a walking skeleton and had lost all of my hair. My family took me to the hospital. I had sores from the top of my head down to my feet. Although I was publicly respected as a teacher, privately I was the greatest of sinners. I could no longer hide my secret: I had visited prostitutes, and I got AIDS as a result. Truly I had reaped what I had sown."

For 4 months, Mohamid was totally bedridden.

Mohamid's family prepared for his funeral, but at that point something miraculous happened. In the hospital Mohamid saw a bright light. *Jesus Christ appeared to him dressed as a doctor, the Great Physician!* The risen Lord Jesus looked at him with love and affection.

"Mohamid, rise up!" Jesus commanded him, just as He spoke to sick people in the Bible.

Mohamid felt confused momentarily, wondering how he could possibly rise up when he was so sick. "But He touched my sick body, took my hand, and sat down next to me on my bed. Jesus seemed to know my every thought."

God's people are filled with compassion. An Ethiopian evangelist showered mercy on Mohamid and took him home to wash his wounds.

"I sensed God was going to use Mohamid for his glory," the evangelist said.

In barely a week, Mohamid was walking again. In his possession is a certificate from his regional general hospital stating that he is no longer HIV-positive. Today Sheik Mohamid Amin is a full-time Christian evangelist and speaks in churches all over Ethiopia, testifying of his healing to the glory of God.

Mohamid's story should emphasize to us the importance of imploring God to visit more people with visions and dreams. As Mohamid himself testifies, "If Jesus had not come to my bed first, I would have lost eternal life, and secondly, I know I would have suffered for an eternity in Hell. There is nothing God cannot do. All of us have done things in the past that we wish we had not done, but God is a present help in trouble. I no longer believe Jesus is just a prophet; now I believe Jesus is the Son of God!"

"A PERSON FULL OF LIGHT"

The New Testament declares that no one can confess Jesus is Lord unless the Holy Spirit enables him to do so. Many people may sincerely believe in Jesus in their hearts, yet they may still be bound spiritually and unable to confess Him as Lord. Sometimes a sinister force seems to try to choke them. A former Muslim, Abd Al-Masih, relates the following fascinating deliverance through a Jesus vision in a simple African pamphlet entitled "Light of Life":

> A Christian organization called *Operation Mobilisation* held a conference for young trainees. They did not easily accept the concept that Muslims live under a collective religious spirit, as was explained by an elder Gospel preacher. Suddenly, an older lady, sitting in the corner, stood up and said: "Your instructor is correct. I was a faithful Muslim and made a personal decision for Christianity. This resulted in severe persecution from my family. I was baptized and became an active member in my church, but I could never bring myself to say, 'Jesus is the Son of God!' I was not really free. Twelve years passed after my decision to believe in Jesus and trust Him as my Savior. I prayed a lot for my complete deliverance and sanctification. Suddenly one night, I saw a person full of light standing near me. In this light, I could see that my whole body was bound with rusty chains. The person in the light touched me and the chains sprang off immediately. Out of my mouth came the cry: 'Jesus, You are the Son of God!'"

She added: "An intellectual acceptance of Jesus does not necessarily result in the regeneration of the heart. A personal act by the Savior, Jesus, was necessary for me to be freed from bondage." This is why it is so important for believers to call upon the Name of the Lord and to invite Him to become active in our lives as our life Guide!

MUSLIM SUPERNATURALLY DELIVERED FROM FEARS OF HELL

In our years of travel throughout Africa, we have encountered and documented many believers who have experienced remarkable visions and dreams about Jesus.

Moussa, from West Africa, the son of an *imam* (mosque leader), was searching for some way of knowing for sure that he was saved. Like many Muslims, he was afraid of going to hell; he was tortured by a promiscuous lifestyle but could not find deliverance from the chains that bound him. Moussa received the Lord not only through studying the Koran, but also by a visitation from "a supernatural being":

I was looking for my salvation like a sick person seeks healing, but I could not find an effective remedy in the Koran. I studied through all of the 114 suras [chapters] of the Koran. I examined them one by one, and there was not one that could tell me *with undeniable certainty* that I would go to Paradise. I was very worried. There was another vital question disturbing me: Are the *Injil* [the Gospels] and the *Torah* [the first five books of the Bible] true or not?

Several times Christians in Abidjan [the capital of the Côte d'Ivoire] tried to preach the Gospel to me. I always replied that their Book had been falsified, because that is what every Muslim is taught to believe. However, this time I wanted to be sure. As usual, after the evening prayer, I opened my Koran to Sura 2, where it says, "Say ye: 'We believe in God, and the revelation given to us, and to Abraham, Ishmael, Isaac, Jacob and the Tribes, and that given to Moses and Jesus, that given to (all) Prophets from their Lord; we made no difference between one and another of them and to Him do we submit.'"

Now I understood that God gave his book to Moses and Jesus. The Koran was therefore telling me not to make any distinction between these books and that of Muslims and to submit myself to the will of God. The commandment of the Koran was clear: I was not to make any difference between these books and the Koran! I was commanded to have faith in them. Would God ask me to believe in a falsified book? Now I was perplexed, because I toed the line and believed that the Bible was corrupt, but the Koran itself was instructing me to obey the Bible.

Moussa continued his meditations in the Koran until he arrived at a verse in the fifth sura (verse 43, or verse 47 in some translations) that says, "But why do they come to thee for decision, when they have (their own) Law before them?"

Moussa noted, "I was being instructed that the Jews couldn't take Mohammed to be a judge or a referee since they have their own Torah.

The lesson I drew from this was that if someone has the Torah, he already has the Word of God. The Torah came from God and therefore contains the Word of God and cannot be corrupt!

"In the same sura, another verse [number 46 in some translations] says, 'And in their footsteps we sent Jesus, the son of Mary, confirming the Law that had come before him. We sent him the Gospel: Therein was guidance and light and confirmation of the Law that had come before him: a guidance and an admonition to those who fear God.'"

Moussa was deeply touched by the fact that the Koran declared that God Himself gave the Gospel to Jesus, and that the Gospel is the guidance and the light for all the people, and that it confirms the book of Moses, the Torah. Thus he even found the confirmation of the Torah and the Gospel in the Koran.

THE HEART OF THE MATTER

Moussa says, "I knew that the main bone of contention, the heart of the matter, was Jesus. Christians say that he is the Son of God, while Muslims say that God did not father any child and that this is not possible. Could God have had a wife in order to have a child? This is blasphemy."

Because of this controversy, Moussa decided to continue his research on the person of Jesus: "Koran commentators agree that 'holy' means 'without sin.' In the 114 suras, I discovered that five titles are attributed to Jesus. These titles are different from those applied to others and are, in fact, greater than the titles of all the others. He is called (1) the Messiah, and (2) the Son of Mary, because nobody knew him to have a human father. Mohammed is called the 'son of Abdullah,' but Jesus is called (3) the Apostle of God, (4) the Spirit of God and (5) the Word of God, one of those close to God, who was honored on this earth and beyond.

"In the 114 suras of the Koran, no sin is attributed to Jesus. Adam's sin can be found in verse 36 [in some translations] of the second sura; the sin of Moses in Sura 28, and Jonah's sin is mentioned in Sura 37. In Sura 40, [verse 55 according to some translations] Mohammed is commanded, 'Ask protection and forgiveness for your fault.'

"I said to myself, 'Even my beloved Mohammed sinned! So how is it that Jesus never sinned? Why is He above all the other prophets?'"

At first Moussa was indignant and jealous for his faith, but he could not help but respect Jesus. He marveled that Jesus had actually lived on this earth for 33 years, and yet there is no record that He ever sinned!

During this time some Christians approached Moussa. They claimed that Jesus was crucified and that their sins had been forgiven as a result of His sacrifice.

"Remember that I was seeking for an assurance of salvation, so I thought their message was too good to be true. I wanted to be sure about it. I opened the Koran to the fourth sura, entitled 'Women': 'They say we killed the Messiah, the Son of Mary. He was not killed, he was not crucified. Another person who resembled him was killed in his stead. God raised a living Jesus into the sky' [verse 156 or 157 according to some translations]."

Now Moussa was relieved to find a verse that contradicted the Christians. The following day, "I opened my Koran to verse 48 of the third sura [or verse 55, according to some translations]. God said, 'Oh Jesus, I will make you taste death. I will raise you unto me, and I will deliver you from the unbelievers and those who follow you will be above those who do not believe in you until the day of resurrection. You will return to me. I will judge your differences.'"

"That verse knocked me out," Moussa recalled emphatically. "It had the effect of a sledge hammer on me. In fact, two elements of that verse conflict with the Cross-denying verse 156/157 of the fourth sura.

> The Koran asserts in the third sura, verse 48 (or 55 according to some translations), "God said to Jesus: 'I will make you taste death, I will raise you unto me.'"

> When I pondered that statement, "I will make you taste death," I said to myself, *This resembles the crucifixion!* And the words, "I will raise you unto me" reminded me of *the resurrection from the dead and Jesus' ascension to Heaven to sit at the right hand of God!*

"And finally, I was astonished that the Koran says that those who follow Jesus Christ are '*above those* who do not follow him *until the day of resurrection.*' The time period specified is not for ten years or forty years or five hundred years, but until the day of resurrection! And since that day has not arrived, was I to accept that Christians were above me? *I was really not ready to accept this revolutionary message that I had found recorded so plainly in my own Koran!*"

During this time, other questions bombarded Moussa's mind, especially concerning the fourth sura, where the crucifixion is denied:

I continued my research and read Sura 19 up to verse 33/34. Jesus Christ, as a small child in his crib, said this: "Peace be with me on the day of my birth, on my place of death, and on my place of resurrection." We accept the fact that peace dwelled with Him from the day of His birth to the day of His resurrection, but not on the day He died because we do not want to accept His death. However, there cannot be resurrection without death. This verse indirectly implies that Jesus Christ was killed and then boldly proclaims He was raised from the dead. I was convinced. *After six months of investigation, I realized that the Koran confirms the Bible and that Jesus Christ is above other prophets. He is the Messiah, the Apostle of God, Mary's son, the Spirit of God, the Word of God. I was furthermore convinced that He was crucified.*"

After all these revelations, Moussa did not know what to do. He was truly immersed in a quandary. To distract his mind, he tried to party in the evenings, but his debauched lifestyle was no longer exciting. He could not eat. He was morose because he knew he was a sinner, and he knew he was not saved.

Therefore, one evening he had the presence of mind to conclude, "If these trials I am going through are of God, then he should prove it to me physically. He should show me what to do."

That evening, he spoke to God in his native language, not in Arabic prayers.

I tried to reason with him like this: "My father is an imam," I said. "When I am with him, I lead the prayers. All my uncles are imams. So I am the descendant of an imam. For that reason, I cannot abandon my religion. I must honor my parents and family." I did not know at that time that Jesus said to His followers that we must love Him more than our families.

I turned off the light, but all of a sudden another light appeared in my room! Someone was there. Initially I was scared, but afterward His presence did not frighten me any longer. The Being approached me and placed His hand on my right shoulder. I remember it as though it happened only yesterday. He spoke to me, saying that all I needed to know had already been revealed to me, and therefore it was my personal decision to believe or not to believe. After this, everything became dark again. I could not sleep the whole night, as I was overwhelmed by the vision and by the choice before me, which He was allowing me to decide by my own free will.

I spent four sleepless nights because I was resisting sleep, but on the fifth day, I could no longer resist. I was overcome by a *deep sleep*. During the deep sleep, I had a dream. I saw a tall man who had blinding bright eyes, like those on car headlights. He tried to dazzle me with this blinding light. I was very much afraid, but suddenly my fear gave way to courage. I demanded to know his name but he would not tell me. Instead he began to recite the Islamic creed. But then he retreated and began to disappear.

I woke up with a startle and realized at that precise moment something in me was stronger than what was in him. I had the impression that there was a change in my life. I concluded that there is no clear-cut promise of salvation in the Koran, but that the Koran clearly declares that the Torah and the Gospel are books from God. I also realized that Jesus is a Prophet above all prophets, that He is sinless, and that He was crucified and raised up again. I had asked God to give me some physical sign. There was the vision, and now this spirit being in my dream was fleeing.

Moussa decided to make a commitment to Jesus Christ. His prayer was so sincere that for the first time he knew that he had really talked with God. He confessed his sins. Suddenly, he closed his eyes and, as in a movie, "I saw passing before my eyes all the sins I had ever committed in night clubs, my indecent sins, the sins of invoking spirits for money, and so on. This vision lasted at least ten minutes, during which time many of my sins passed before my eyes. But I also knew that Jesus Christ had entered my life and that it was He who had given me forgiveness of all those sins and an indescribable joy."

Jesus Christ proved that He alone had the power to deliver Moussa from life-controlling sins.

"I thank God for giving me the strength to say 'yes' to the truth proclaimed by the Bible. Now I want to ask my dear Muslim friends: What are you going to do with Jesus? Will you go to the side of the One who is the Truth, Jesus Christ, who assures you of salvation now and in the hereafter? Do not say, 'Because my father is Muslim, I am also a Muslim.' God has no grandchildren. He only has sons. Ask yourself whether you are saved. If you die today, where will you spend eternity? That is the question you *must* answer. You will find uncertainties in the Koran, whereas the Bible, which is confirmed by the Koran, shows you the path above all others, the only path. The Bible tells you plainly that Jesus is the Door to God. The important thing is for your sins to be forgiven, and the only way for that to happen is through the cleansing of the Blood of the Savior, Jesus. He forgives all your sins, even those you have committed in childhood."

SPECIAL INVITATION

I especially want to say to any Muslim friends who may be reading this testimony and this book: if you are experiencing dreams or visions about Jesus, if you are seeing a Man in White, be assured that He is trying to communicate information of the greatest importance concerning your free salvation and acceptance by God through the atoning Blood of Jesus. Please do not resist Him. Please do not be alarmed, but pray and ask for more revelation.

Jesus always says, "Come! Follow Me." He gives you this open invitation in Revelation 3:20: "Behold, I stand at the door, and knock: if any man hear My voice, and open the door, I will come in to him, and will sup with him, and he with Me."

In Israel I met a former Shia Muslim who had become a believer in Jesus through a supernatural encounter in Iran, where he was born. He told me that one of the greatest burdens he experienced as a Muslim was guilt because he could never faithfully pray five times a day—especially the prayer during the night. But after he became a follower of Jesus, he was delivered from religious baggage because the laws of God were written by the Holy Spirit upon his heart. As a believer in Jesus, he could enjoy a perfect, guilt-free night's sleep for the first time in his life.

In Matthew 11:28, Jesus gives this special invitation to all who are burdened by sin and by religious law: "Come unto Me, all ye that labor and are heavy laden, and I will give you rest."

CHAPTER 6

Glory in Egypt

The burden of Egypt. Behold the Lord rideth upon a swift cloud and shall come into Egypt...for they shall cry unto the Lord because of the oppressors and He shall send them a saviour, and a great one, and He shall deliver them. And the Lord shall be known to Egypt, and the Egyptians shall know the Lord.... In that day shall there be a highway out of Egypt to Assyria. In that day shall ...Israel be the third with Egypt and with Assyria, even a blessing in the midst of the land: Whom the Lord of hosts shall bless, saying, "Blessed be Egypt My people, and Assyria the work of My hands, and Israel Mine inheritance" (Selected verses from Isaiah chapter 19).

The Lord's glory cloud will descend swiftly into Egypt. He has already sent the Savior, a mighty one, Jesus the Redeemer of Egypt. As a young refugee in Egypt with His parents, who fled from the tyrant King Herod, it is likely that Jesus took His first steps in Egypt. By His footsteps, He claimed the jewel of Africa for His Kingdom long ago.

Providentially, the Lord will increasingly make Himself known to Egypt, and the Egyptians will increasingly receive personal, saving knowledge of the Lord. He promises to smite and then to heal Egypt, and they will return to the Lord, who is *YHWH*, the King of the Universe.

A highway of peace and prosperity will stretch from Egypt through Israel to Iraq. These three nations, according to the Amplified Bible's rendition of Isaiah 19:25, will be incorporated into a "messianic league" of religious and financial prosperity that will bless the entire world. "Egypt, my people; Assyria, the work of my hands; and Israel my inheritance" are three countries that are promised in Scripture national salvation and "most favored nation" status in the Kingdom of God! These traditional enemies will ultimately find unity, not in politics, but in the Messiah!

For a number of years, our ministry teams have been traversing this "Isaiah 19" highway to prepare the way of the Lord. He has imparted strategies and a "heavenly pattern" for us to organize bold open-air meetings in Egypt, Israel, and Iraq. As we have preached and distributed Bibles and *Jesus* videos, we have blown the trumpet of the Lord from Cairo to Baghdad! Truly, the Messiah Yeshua is coming soon to take the reins of this volatile region, and He will possess a Biblical rod of iron to command all nations to live in peace. He will dispense justice to the Palestinians and to all the oppressed peoples of the Middle East as well as the entire world! Every corrupt leader and every tyrant will be judged.

GOSPEL TENT AT THE PYRAMIDS

One of the greatest ministry doors the Lord has opened for our Exploits Ministry was the first Gospel tent at the Pyramids in 2001 with official permission from the Egyptian government! As many as 50 Muslims prayed with us as I preached a strong Gospel message at a banquet in our peace tent at the Pyramids. Because the event was surrounded with heavy security and police, we were not free to call these Egyptians forward publicly. Nevertheless, many of them later testified to my husband and me and to other team members that they had prayed in the tent service to receive Jesus.

"Why am I shaking all over?" said one of the Muslim attendants to my husband at the tent event. "Because," he explained, "the Holy Spirit is upon you to confirm that Jesus is present."

The Pyramids Gospel tent was birthed in a vision I had experienced during an earlier ministry trip to Cairo. While deep in agonizing prayer for the souls in the Middle East, I suddenly saw myself enlarging the stakes of a white "Tabernacle of David" at the Pyramids. I had already been speaking to some Egyptian pastors about sponsoring an open-air meeting, but they did not want to take that chance and had invited me instead to hold an event on a "safe" ministry compound behind walls and gates.

But in the vision, Jesus strengthened my hands as I drove the tent stakes into the Egyptian sand. Then He looked into my eyes sternly as *if* to say, "I want no foolishness from you. Get me this tent!" However, the only word He *actually* spoke to me in the vision was, "obsequiousness." (The Lord sometimes speaks economically in dreams and visions with words beyond my vocabulary. I must look for them in a dictionary to fully understand the dream.)

I couldn't wait to visit a bookstore at the airport to look up "obsequiousness," meaning "excessively eager to please, fawning, groveling, men-pleasing." Jesus was therefore commanding me not to be a man-pleaser! He showed me how to receive permission for the Gospel tent.

That evening as we drove to the tabernacle in the shadow of the Great Pyramid, the beautiful tent was like a dream, a mirage in the desert, but it was reality! With God *all* things are possible! Egyptian horsemen greeted us, blowing long silver trumpets. One of the most anointed praise teams in the Middle East provided worship songs.

An internationally known preacher had opined that the date of the Pyramids tent event "was a trap." This was a test for me to pass—either to listen to a human being, or to go ahead with the guidance I had already received from the Lord. The event was held the day before riots broke out in Cairo, and if we had staged the tent event 24 hours later, hardly any Egyptian would have attended because of fear and security measures.

A great woman in Cairo, a Coptic Christian filled with the Holy Spirit, helped us to organize the first Gospel tent at the Pyramids. She wrote the following Christmas greeting concerning other supernatural phenomena occurring in this Bible land:

> God is working mighty signs and wonders in Egypt. In the town of Assiyout, one of the towns where Jesus lived as a baby while in Egypt, there are heavenly brilliant lights appearing on top of the church of St. Mark in the darkness of the night. [St. Mark was the apostle to Egypt.] In addition there appear Holy Ghost doves in bright florescent-like light flying high in the sky. I had the privilege of going and seeing for myself. Hundreds of thousands of people of all faiths have been flocking every night to see these signs since August 17. It was announced in a BBC broadcast from London on September 6. Many are miraculously healed. God is telling His people in Egypt that in spite of much tribulation and persecution, He will never leave us or forsake us.

> It is also a power encounter. If you will recall recent events in the news, in this town there was much violence against God's people by Islamic fanatics. Today people of all faiths come...even the police are helping to organize the visits. Many will never believe except when they see signs and wonders.

> God revealed to me His special plan for Egypt. Like in the days of old, when the people of Israel came to Egypt to seek bread during the time of Joseph, so God is sending a famine on the Middle East, according to Amos 8:13: "not a famine of bread, nor a thirst for water, but of hearing the words of the Lord." Isaiah 19:20 says, "He shall send them a saviour, and a great one, and He shall deliver them." The Savior like Joseph is a picture of Jesus and His body, the true Church. Like Joseph, who was filled with the spirit of God and His

wisdom, so will be the Church, and as a result there will be an exchange of authority from Pharaoh, the god of this world, to the Church. In Genesis 41:42, "Pharaoh took off his ring from his hand, and put it upon Joseph's hand," so Egypt will again feed the other countries with the Bread of life. Isaiah 19:23 foresees a highway out of Egypt to Assyria and Israel. That is why God says, "Blessed be Egypt My people." So please pray for revival in Egypt.

According to many of my independent sources in Egypt, a number of believers in Jesus from a Muslim background have come to faith through supernatural, unconventional means. One Egyptian Muslim was reading the *Injil* (Gospel) when he came to Luke 3, describing the descent of the Holy Spirit in the form of a dove onto Jesus. And God said, "This is my son in whom I am well pleased." As the Muslim read those words, a stormy wind broke into his room and a voice spoke to him, "I am Jesus Christ, whom you hate. I am the Lord whom you are looking for." The Spirit fell upon the Egyptian; he wept , and Jesus entered into his heart from that moment.

FAITH TO MOVE MOUNTAINS

Egypt has always been associated with supernatural signs and wonders. It was in the land of Egypt that some of the most awesome Bible signs were wrought under the rod of Moses. Egyptians hunger for the supernatural, and one of the greatest miracles in the Middle Eastern church was purportedly accomplished in Egypt. Many Egyptian Christians (and some Muslims as well) believe the following account to be historical fact:

According to Coptic traditional sayings, the tenth Century Fatimid Caliph Al Muizz, an enlightened man, often invited religious leaders to debate in his presence.

In one of those meetings Pope Abram, the spiritual leader of the Orthodox Egyptian Christians, debated an adversary named Jacob Ibn Killis. The Coptic Pope waxed eloquent in the debate. Plotting to take revenge, Ibn Killis quoted the New Testament verse in which Jesus declared, "If ye have faith as a grain of mustard seed, ye shall say unto this mountain, Remove hence to yonder place; and it shall remove; and nothing shall be impossible unto you" (Matthew 17:20).

The Caliph demanded that the Coptic Pope demonstrate the veracity of his faith by means of moving the Mokattam Mountain. (The Caliph saw a practical opportunity to remove the Mokattam, which was spoiling his view. At the same time, if the Copts proved powerless, it would signify that the Christian religion was false, and they could be destroyed.)

And so the believers took the Biblical pattern found in the Book of Esther. After three days of earnest prayer and fasting by Christians throughout the land of Egypt, they chose a simple shoemaker named Simon, known for his humility and faith, to command the mountain to move. At that time, the Coptic Christians made their livelihoods in handicrafts. Simon worked in one of the crafts widespread in Old Cairo and still known in the bazaars: tanning hides for use in making shoes and leather goods.

Simon simply believed that mountains could literally be moved, just as the Bible says! Under his faith commands, a great earthquake swept over the mountain. Each time the people stood up to worship, the mountain was thrust upward, and the rising sun could be seen shining underneath it. When the people sat down, the mountain thrust down. This was repeated three times, and because of this miracle, the mountain was moved and the Christian community was saved.

Simon was never seen again. It was popularly believed that he disappeared to avoid receiving glory or credit for the miracle. Today in Egypt he is beloved by Christians and many Muslims as Saint Simon the Tanner—Saint Sama'an, in Arabic—and a monastery was dedicated to Simon nearly a thousand years after his mountain-moving miracle.

Today the monastery and a beautiful cave cathedral lie behind Zabbalin, a village of garbage collectors. This village was established in 1969 when Cairo garbage collectors, many of whom are cultural Christians, were moved to one of the hills of the miracle Mokattam Mountain.

At the far end of the "garbage" village an unexpected, stunning place awaits visitors: a vast open space like a Christian theme park, with dramatic colored carvings by a Polish artist decorating the miracle mountain. The artwork presents stories from the Bible, such as the Holy Family's journey to Egypt. The main cathedral is named after Saint Simon to commemorate the transfer of Mokattam Mountain in November 1979. The power of God is said to be moving there. The believers in Egypt are crying out to God for major miracles to happen again in their land, and so the following report should not be surprising.

EGYPT EXPERIENCES A GREAT MODERN SIGN AND WONDER

An Arab friend in the Old City of Jerusalem exclaimed to me excitedly, "All of Egypt is crazy [stirred] over a miracle!"

I confirmed the validity of the miracle with a high-ranking Egyptian Coptic priest who lives in London. I also telephoned Cairo to confirm the validity of the sign and wonder, which occurred in Egypt and which was reported throughout the Middle East, even on TV, according also to a reliable Egyptian pastor.

"The report of which you have heard," said my Cairo friend, "is very widespread in Egypt. Everybody—and that certainly includes the Muslims—is discussing it like wildfire. Some in the Church are skeptical and, in fact, have always been skeptical of miracles! But our God is well able to do these things, because there is a great, great hunger in Egypt for the reality of God's presence and miracles."

According to the report, an Egyptian man murdered his sister-in-law in order to inherit family money. He decided to bury her children alive with her corpse to prevent the children from inheriting the money.

Miraculously, ten days later the two children were rescued and their uncle was apprehended. A reporter interviewed both the murderer in prison and also one of the rescued children. The following amazing details were heard in the account on TV, according to my Egyptian sources:

Two children were incarcerated in a tomb and abandoned to die by their cruel uncle. [Many poor people actually live in the mausoleums of Cairo in the so-called City of the Dead.] A passerby heard their noise and rescued them. How did they survive ten days without food and water?

To this, the older child replied, "Every evening a man came and woke up my Mother, and she would give milk for the baby. Streams of light were shining from this man. He also gave me dates to eat." (Date pips were reportedly found in the tomb; and it is a recorded fact that many Christian monks have subsisted for years in the desert with only dates for food.)

The reporter asked, "Who was this man that could cause a dead Mother to produce milk to feed her baby?"

The child answered, " I don't know his name, but he had two holes in his hands with blood streaming out of the holes!"

At that point, the interviewer gasped, "Do you realize you are describing the Prophet Issa [the Islamic name for Jesus]?" Suddenly, the television program was abruptly ended and the screen went blank momentarily. Nevertheless, Egypt has not stopped talking about this miracle.

Following are comments from an Egyptian minister who verified that the miracle was reported on TV:

The story, which potentially may have been seen by millions of people, was not repeated by the news media, which is absolutely not a surprise if you understand the Middle East. Part of the miracle is that the story *was* seen on TV! You have to understand that if the station doing the interview knew what this child was going to say, I seriously doubt the story would have been aired in the first place, and most likely the government cut it off immediately from airing again or getting into the papers.

Just as you can be sure a story like this (or any of the countless miracles that our Lord does around the world) will not get into the Western press because of the liberal, ungodly media (and predictable Western skepticism even among Christians), the media of the Arab world is strictly censored, and so this report had to be a big "oops" for them. Jesus still heals the sick, gives sight to the blind, and raises the dead, at least in places where people are desperate enough to need Him and simple enough to believe Him when He shows up.

Workers in the Middle East will tell you that most Muslims who receive Christ have had a dream, vision, or actual visitation of the Lord, enabling them to overcome the fear and oppression. This is happening by the thousands, but we're not likely to hear about it on the news.

My Egyptian ministry associate added, "If nothing else, I hope people are encouraged to keep praying for the miracles, dreams, and visions that confirm the life-giving Word of our Lord and Savior. Be of good cheer, He has overcome the world!"

REVIVAL UNDER FATHER ZECHARIAH

In a nation of more than 60 million, Egyptian Christians of different denominations comprise 10 percent of the population. The Coptic (Egyptian Christian church) is by far the largest body of Christians in the Middle East and is a strategic key for evangelism in the region. The Copts are an apostolic church founded by St. Mark and headed by the Coptic Pope, a deeply spiritual man. The Pope can be visited at his weekly Bible studies with a question and answer session at Cairo's Coptic Cathedral. St. Mark the Evangelist's tomb is enshrined in Alexandria, Egypt.

All of Egypt would believe in Jesus as Lord if they were free—not just "on paper"—to openly follow Him, according to a banished Coptic priest. Father Zechariah, leader of a revival in Egypt and a great lover of all the peoples of the Middle East, still preaches to his beloved homeland daily via satellite from outside the country. Father Zechariah is becoming well known through his Gospel broadcasts, and many Muslims watch him because he knows the Koran and their culture and how to reach them. He is very bold. Pray for his daily protection!

Dressed in the long black robe of a Coptic priest and holding a wooden cross in his animated hands, Father Zechariah is a delightfully humorous, humble servant of the Most High God.

During a TV interview that we conducted for British TV, Father Zechariah described the revival in Egypt. It began with his thirst for God and a terrible vision of multitudes of souls plunging into hell.

However, when Father Zechariah became a priest, he did not personally know the Savior.

> I grew up in a religious family, and I must differentiate between "religious" and a real believer. Routinely we would fast and go to church, and as a teenager I was asked to teach in Sunday school in our Orthodox Church. I tried to please God through fasting and personal efforts. I graduated with a B.A. from university and worked as a teacher in high school, and at the age of 59 I was ordained as a priest.
>
> I was motivated by great zeal like Saul of Tarsus to protect and propagate teachings of the Orthodox Church, but all of that zeal did not quench my thirst of trying to please God. When reading the Bible, I always discarded verses that talked about faith because I did not want to be associated with Protestants.
>
> In my spiritual search, I visited our country's famous and ancient monasteries. I saw in a library 38 volumes of the teachings of our early Egyptian church fathers. My hopes were set on these teachings to find the answer to my longings. Through the help of a generous American doctor, I was able to buy the 38 volumes. So I devoted myself to searching and studying these books in the hopes of understanding salvation.
>
> Through the writings of St. Cyril and St. Clement, I came to realize that salvation is by faith through grace! Furthermore I came to understand the place for discipline and good works—that these are fruit of the Spirit—but that only Jesus could save me. As an ordained priest, for the first time in my

life, I knelt down and asked Christ to come into my life as Savior and Redeemer.

HOW THE REVIVAL BEGAN

I asked Father Zechariah how the Revival began, and he gave an answer that is true to all revivals—it began first with himself.

> I had read in the books of our early Church fathers that all believers should possess a very essential gift and anointing—that we should be anointed by the Holy Spirit and have a Spirit-filled life. I started to pray, and I fasted for three days, asking God to fill me with the Holy Spirit and to use me. Before the first day of the revival, I was alone praying, and the voice of God started a debate with me.
>
> "Why do you want to be anointed?" the Voice asked.
>
> "To bring people to you."
>
> "Are you sure this is your only motive? What about your reputation? Do you want to be known as an anointed man who wins people to God?"
>
> I said, "God, you know me well, and if I will misuse this gift, please don't give it to me. I don't want anything but your glory." Then I stopped praying because I knew that he knows I am a proud person, and so I assumed he would not bless me.
>
> "Do you believe I can change hearts of people to bring them to salvation?" the Voice continued to ask.
>
> "Of course! That is why I prayed to you to change the hearts of people!"
>
> "Can I change the hearts of people, but I cannot change your heart? If you are self-centered and you feel you are proud, why don't you ask me to change your attitude and purify your heart?"
>
> "Good," I said, brightening with fresh courage, "Do that please—purify my intentions, my heart, my everything.

Do what is essential to bring people to you, and if you find me unworthy, find someone else, because the people are in need of you."

After that soul-baring encounter, the evangelist priest experienced a horrifying vision:

People were like sheep walking on top of a mountain, and they were falling off the edge down into the valley into *fire, fire, fire*. I found myself crying, "Please, God, help! Don't let those sheep go down into this fire. People are going to hell! Send whomever you send, but please, God, save those people!"

And that visionary experience was the key to the blessing. I praise God for his generous gift, and I believe that a power came over me, and when I went to preach, honestly, I forgot what I had prepared for the sermon. I know only the main aim was to communicate salvation, and we knew only that we want God to save the people! What I *could* remember very well were tears from me and from the congregation. We were weeping and crying under the influence of the Holy Spirit. And many people from that day started to repent and to ask for righteousness from Jesus, asking for the blood of Jesus Christ to purify them. And on that day the revival started.

As God said in the last chapter of Mark—these are good verses—"These signs will accompany those who believe. In my name they will drive out demons, they will speak in new tongues, they will pick up snakes and when they drink deadly poison it will not hurt them. They will place their hands on sick people and they will get well. These signs will accompany those who believe, and God was proving his message by the miracles that followed."

MUSLIMS VISIT CHURCH TO BE HEALED

Father Zechariah continues:

So I asked God to prove his message to the people. When I was going to the church one day, I found a man in the courtyard

lying on the ground and crying. I told the people to
into the church and I started to pray. I didn't know at ι
that God had given me a special gift for healing, so ι
"Please, God, heal your son; he's suffering. Please help n
mercy on him."

Then the demon-possessed boy waked up and hugged me.
He cried, "Thank God! I had a heavy load on my back and
now it is very light; I don't feel anything!" He was possessed
and now healed. After that I found in the church many
Muslims coming every day to be healed!

I moved to Cairo, specifically to Heliopolis, which the Bible
tells us will be one of the five cities in Egypt that will know
the language of God. There God gave us a wonderful time, a
revival for about 15 years. I did not go with the intention to
reach Muslims, but God sent all these people to my church
to accept Jesus Christ! The Bible predicts that God will say
in the future, "Blessed be my people Egypt." Yes, we will see
it. Muslims are now ready to accept the Good News of Jesus
Christ if there is freedom and respect for human rights.

There were miracles of healing the sick and exorcisms.
Those who were possessed by devils were healed—sure!—
because any heart empty of Christ and the Holy Spirit is
vulnerable to the devil. So many of them came to be healed,
and he who is healed accepts Jesus Christ! I wrote books
about Christianity to make bridges. One of these books con-
cerns the Trinity because I found a verse in the Koran that
mentions all three Persons of the Holy Trinity—God, the
Word [Jesus] and the Spirit.

VISIT FROM AN ARABIAN PRINCE

Father Zechariah illustrates the healing power of the Trinity with
this story:

A Prince from Arabia came to meet me. God sent him to
me. I told you that I don't go to people, but God sends

people to me! Just as in the Bible, Ananias was a disciple in Damascus, but God sent Saul to Damascus to him. So this Arabian prince came to me with four attendants, but he wanted to share and to speak privately. He said, "I was in my country and I was not sleeping. With my own eyes I saw a person come into my room with a long beard and a big cross and stand in front of me. After a while he disappeared. Who do you think that man was?"

So first I asked him, "What did *you* think?"

He answered, "In our belief we have *jinn* [good spirits and bad spirits—devils] and I think he was one of them—a *jinn*."

I told him, "According to our religion, there is no good and bad devils; all devils are bad; all of them are called satan." [There are three potential sources of dreams and visions— God, one's own self and demonic influences.]

So I explained to him, "This vision was not a *jinn*; it is a true vision of a messenger from God, maybe a saint, coming with the Cross, saying to you that the Cross is the way." [It is also likely that the vision could have been of Father Zechariah himself, since the prince's description sounded like the Coptic evangelist!]

The prince mused, "There is another thing I want to ask you."

"You are welcome," I replied.

"You know that I am religious and I pray always asking for God's help, and I have a brother who has no children. I pray always that God will give them children, and I had a dream. A voice spoke to me in the dream and asked, 'Do you want your brother and sister-in-law to be healed?' The voice said, 'If you say, "In the name of the Father, and the Son and the Holy Spirit," they will be healed.' I was very afraid."

I asked the prince, "Why were you afraid? Did you think the Father, the Son and the Holy Spirit are three different gods, and you believe in only one God?"

The prince was silent. At this point I opened the Koran and said, "Look at this verse, found in the 'Woman's Chapter,' [verse 171 in some translations]: 'Jesus Christ is the messenger of God and he is his Word and he is the Spirit of him.' So, I tell you, God is a person, and he has a Word and a Spirit. Jesus Christ is the Word, and the Spirit is the Holy Spirit. So we believe in one God, the holy Trinity. Human beings are also a trinity—you have a body, you have a mind, and you also have a spirit—three parts in one person."

I did not ask the Prince to believe in Jesus or not to believe in Jesus, but the prince pressed me. "Can I have a Bible?"

I answered, "Yes, you're welcome, but you know the Bible may be difficult to understand." So the prince asked me for an explanation. I gave him a commentary on the Bible that explains how to apply the verses.

He said, "Thank you very much. This is precious. Where are the Psalms? Can I pray with the Psalms?"

"Yes!"

"Is there any reward from God for praying with these?"

"Yes, there is every blessing in the heavens," I said. He was very happy.

JESUS HEALS A MUSLIM PARALYTIC

The Lord was proving His presence by healing the sick and casting out devils as teams from Father Zechariah's church visited hospitals and orphanages. As was their custom, they prayed with their Christian brethren and did not impose their beliefs on the Muslims. But there was a very spiritually hungry Muslim man in a Cairo hospital who had been involved in an accident and was paralyzed.

While the believers from my church were praying in the hospital for a Christian, this paralyzed young Muslim man—his name was Abed—demanded with indignation, "Why don't you pray for me?"

They said, "We will have to ask the priest. Don't put us in trouble because you are not a Christian."

So I said to them, "I myself will go and pray for him," and I went.

Abed said to me, "Those people came and prayed for *that* man and gave *him* some books. But why didn't they give any books to *me*? Why didn't they pray for *me*? Could they not see that I also am in need?"

I said, "You know that we are not supposed to preach to Muslims."

"No!" Abed shouted with great frustration, "I *asked* for that, and now I am asking you to pray for me and to give me those books!"

So I prayed for him. And when I prayed for him (remember his legs were dead—they were not moving at all), suddenly he started to move his toes!

"Look! I can feel!" Abed screamed.

"Praise God," I said, "it's because of your faith."

Abed was not totally healed at this point, but the numbness had disappeared and feeling had returned to his legs.

"Where are the books?" the man demanded hungrily.

So I gave him the Gospel of St. John. The next day he called me, "Please, I have finished the book. Where is the other?"

I gave him the whole Bible, and then he asked me to send him some people to take him to our meetings. So he used to come every Tuesday and Thursday in his wheelchair, and the brothers took him back to the hospital.

One day he came to me and said, "I read that a believer should be baptized, and I want to be baptized."

I said, "You are welcome. Come." I took him to the baptism room, and I prepared to put [sprinkle] water on him.

"No!" the new believer demanded again with indignation. "Do you baptize all the people like that?"

Father Zechariah explained that they normally baptize by immersion in the Egyptian Coptic Church but that it was too difficult to immerse a man in a wheelchair.

But Abed would not accept half measures. He wanted a proper baptism.

"He said forcefully to me, 'I should go down in the water like all the others.' So we managed somehow to help him down into the baptism pool. He was baptized and came out."

After one month Abed announced to the priest, "I had a vision. You came and all the brothers and sisters came with you, and you held my hand and said to me, 'In the name of Jesus, walk!' and I walked twelve steps. So please come and pray."

Abed had been paralyzed for two years and the muscles in his legs were atrophied. But Father Zechariah obeyed the vision and commanded Abed to walk in the name of Jesus. He got up and walked exactly twelve steps and then asked again for his wheelchair. He fulfilled the vision as far as the vision went.

But after another month, Abed visited Father Zechariah again and announced, "Today I will walk for good. Pray for me!" So after the prayer, he left the wheelchair and rolled it back to the hospital. All the people said, "Why aren't you in the chair?"

"I don't need it! Jesus Christ healed me!"

"What?" the people cried. "Have you become a Christian?"

"Why not? He healed me! Why not?"

Whenever events explode like another episode in the Book of the Acts of the Apostles, no matter in what country, the genuine work of the Lord will surely be challenged!

PRISON BECOMES VISIONARY PALACE

Father Zechariah insists, "We never attacked any religion or anybody because we in Christianity are honor-bound to love everybody in the world. All people are the creatures of God." Nevertheless, he was imprisoned twice—the first time for nearly a year. He was accused of forcing people to convert: "But we never forced anybody. Sharing the Gospel is not forcing. I must do my work. According to the Bible, I must fulfill the commandment to go to all the nations, to preach, teach, and baptize all the nations. So I did not do anything outside of my Bible. And God should be obeyed above all persons."

During his first imprisonment, the evangelist priest was incarcerated with three others in a cell that measured one meter and a half by one meter and 18 centimeters with no running water, no windows—"very miserable conditions"—but "Praise God," Father Zechariah recalled, "He gave us strength. When I was sleeping the ceiling of the cell was as high as the sky, and I also found the walls to be like a palace. On the ground it was [as if I could see and feel] thick, beautiful carpet and the [visionary] furniture was very ornate. I spent my first day in God's palace. He transported me and invited me to stay there, and after that, I did not feel the narrowness of my cell because I experienced the width of God's palace."

The second and last imprisonment lasted only four days:

> This time they put me in solitary confinement, and they did not give me food or water. They said, "If you want to eat or drink you have to change your [priestly] garments and wear prison clothes."

> But because I know the law, I said, "I'm not charged and sentenced yet. My case is under investigation, so I have to wear my own clothes."

> They said, "So let your clothes give you food."

> I said, "Thank you, because my Father gives me food, daily food." But God called me to fast and to go four days without

food and water, and on the fourth day the police commanded me to leave the cell.

Suddenly the door opened and the police said, "Get your clothes and come!"

I said, "I have no clothes; only what I am wearing."

They said, "Then get your food and come."

I said, "I have no food because you have given me nothing to eat or to drink for four days."

They said, "Then come with yourself and let's go."

Outside in the refreshing air a high-ranking policeman ordered the priest, "Quickly, get into my car!"

Then the police officer pressed Father Zechariah: "Tell me, who is the man that is backing you? Because whoever he is, he is a very powerful person!"

"Yes, I know He's powerful!"

"Who is he? Where is he?"

Father Zechariah looked out of the window of the black Mercedes to the clear blue sky and mused, "He dwells in a blue tent."

"Where's this blue tent?" the policeman demanded.

"*This* blue tent," Zechariah reiterated, pointing up to the expansive sky.

The faithful priest was transported to the office of the secret police, who said, "Welcome. You are now an ambassador of Egypt in Australia. You are now released by the order of the President himself. Go and speak well of Egypt!"

Isaiah chapter 19, quoted at the beginning of this chapter, foresees the coming national salvation of Egypt.

How will it happen that, according to the Bible, all Egypt will know the Lord? No doubt, supernatural events such as those quoted in these pages will summon the people's attention to Jesus.

According to revivalist Zechariah, "Egypt is open to accept the Lordship of Jesus. They are very thirsty and hungry; the only hindrance is lack of freedom. At this point, the Muslim who is converted to Christianity openly would be persecuted or killed, so they are afraid. When they come to Christ they come secretly, but there are even now some who are willing to pay the price of martyrdom.

"I believe God is blessing Egypt this way—many people come to Christ secretly through books, Bibles, satellites, and through the Internet. Muslims hear and study and they receive Jesus into their hearts. So I believe that this secret movement will be hidden until most of the people accept Jesus Christ.

"And when they are finally open with one another, they will discover that all of Egypt has become Christian!"

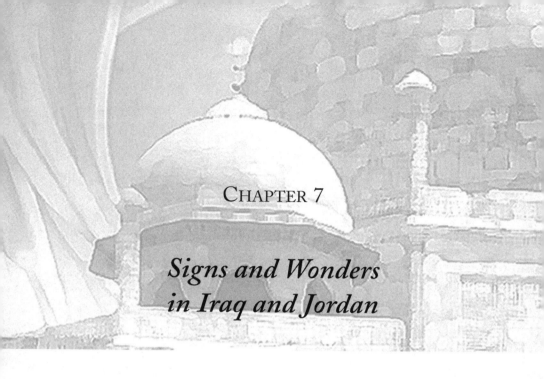

CHAPTER 7

Signs and Wonders in Iraq and Jordan

In the former "no-fly" zone of Iraq, two Muslim leaders experienced independent visions in which they both saw the risen Son of God. Jesus appeared before them in glory, declaring that He is Jesus and that they were to seek the Truth. Overcome by His presence, they both fell to their knees in awe and worship.

Days later, in separate locations, the two Muslim clerics were given the opportunity to watch the *Jesus* film on video. The actor who portrays Jesus resembled the man they had seen in their vision. Both clerics prayed, gave their lives to the Lord and days later "happened" to meet one another. They now lead a group of 17 other new believers who have all experienced a vision of the risen Christ. (This information comes from the *Jesus* Film Project.) These are not isolated instances. There have been other reports on numerous occasions.

The Holy Spirit is hovering over the Hashemite Kingdom of Jordan in a special way. There is an open Heaven of revelation every time we are privileged to visit Jordan. Our ministry team conducted a remarkable bold Jericho March in 1999 in Jordan accompanied by signs and wonders in the northern part of the country, where Jesus cast out the legion of demons from the demonized man, and in the south in Petra. We will see revival break out in Jordan sooner rather than later. Many of the signs and wonders in the Arab world sprung from a revival in the Trans-Jordan region of the Holy Land in 1933.

In neighboring Iraq, the Spirit of God is moving mightily as He is preparing to fulfill the Messianic period of universal peace mentioned in Isaiah 19:23-25, when Assyria (Iraq) will become "the work of the Lord's hands." A highway of holiness will stretch from Egypt through Israel all the way to Iraq. All borders will be open as all the peoples of the Middle East worship the Lord of Hosts!

There are many reasons why Iraq is important to God and why His Spirit is moving there through visions and dreams at this time. Iraq was the cradle of civilization. The patriarch Abraham hailed from Ur of the Chaldeans, which was located in modern Iraq, and Noah built his famous ark in Iraq. The Tower of Babel was also located there. The patriarch Jacob returned to his forebear's roots in Iraq to find his wife Rachel. And, of course, the most famous rebellious preacher Jonah was commissioned by God to preach a revival in Nineveh, which was located in northern Iraq (today Nineveh is called Mosul).

Assyria (Iraq) conquered the ten tribes of Israel. Babylon, which today is still a province of Iraq, destroyed Jerusalem under the leadership of the Babylonian King Nebuchadnezzar. Other famous Bible incidents occurred in Iraq: three Hebrews who eschewed idol worship were thrown into a fiery furnace but survived because of a Christophany in Iraq (an appearance of Jesus as the fourth person in the fire).

The prophet Daniel survived persecution in the lions' den. Babylonian King Nebuchadnezzar received dreams concerning the history of the world and Daniel interpreted them. Babylonian King Belshazzar beheld terrifying supernatural "writing on the wall" from the hand of God. And the prophet Ezekiel received outstanding visions concerning important spiritual realities and prophecies while he was a captive in Iraq.

In the New Testament, we discover that wise men traveled from Iraq to find the baby Jesus, and the Apostle Peter preached in Iraq. The following e-mail has been sent around the world:

> Israel is the nation most often mentioned in the Bible. But do you know which nation is second? It is Iraq! However, that is not the name that is used in the Bible. The names used in the Bible are Assyria, Babylon, Land of Shinar, and Mesopotamia. The word "Mesopotamia" means "between the two rivers," more exactly between the Tigris and Euphrates Rivers. The name *Iraq* means "country with deep roots." Indeed Iraq is a country with deep roots and is a very significant country in the Bible. Here's why:
>
> - Eden was in Iraq—Genesis 2:10-14
> - Adam and Eve were created in Iraq—Genesis 2:7-8
> - Satan made his first recorded appearance in Iraq—Genesis 3:1-6
> - Nimrod established Babylon and the Tower of Babel was built in Iraq—Genesis 10:8-9; 11:1-4
> - The confusion of the languages took place in Iraq—Genesis 11:5-11
> - Abraham came from a city in Iraq—Genesis 11:31; Acts 7:2-4
> - Isaac's bride came from Iraq—Genesis 24:3-4, 10
> - Jacob spent 20 years in Iraq—Genesis 27:43-45; 31:38
> - The first world empire was in Iraq—Daniel 1:1-2; 2:36-38
> - The greatest revival in history was in a city in Iraq—Jonah 3
> - The book of Nahum was a prophecy against a city in Iraq—Nahum
> - The book of Revelation contains prophecies against Babylon, which was the old name for the nation of Iraq—Revelation 17 & 18

No other nation, except Israel, has more history and prophecy associated with it than Iraq.

Likewise, because the present-day Hashemite Kingdom of Jordan is part of the original Holy Land of God, I believe it is especially open to the Gospel and to new visitations of the Holy Spirit. Our ministry's visit to the rock-hewn city of Petra was one of the most supernatural events we have ever experienced as a team. The Holy Spirit met us there with awesome intercessory travail as well as end-time visions of the Jewish people fleeing to Petra. The late King Hussein was often seen in visions and dreams of various Arab believers as one who was a friend of the Church of Jesus Christ.

Throughout many cultures of the East, Africa, and the Middle East, the ability to conceive children is extremely important. Barren couples have received prayer to conceive children in our Gospel reconciliation outreaches, and they have reported joyously the births of healthy children as a result of believing prayer in the name of Jesus.

In our ministry outreaches we have distributed the videos and DVDs of the *Miracles* documentaries filmed in Jordan by CBN TV that carefully recount many modern miracles in this Holy Land. Among these miracles is the report of a Jordanian man with a withered arm who was healed in a dream by Jesus. Nobody was more surprised than the handicapped man when he awakened to see that the dream had already become reality! He ran excitedly throughout Amman proclaiming that Jesus is alive and that He still heals today!

One of the *Miracles* documentaries produced by CBN that we also distribute in our outreaches documents the true story of a barren woman desperate for children who received from Jesus the miraculous ability to conceive. Today she is a happy mother and homemaker.

Childless Iraqi Woman Conceives

Another childless woman who told me her testimony personally was increasingly saddened as the months and years passed without her being able to bear any children. But one night, to her surprise and amazement, she saw a vision of Jesus. She was momentarily frightened by such an unexpected visitation. Rays of light emanated from His compassionate face. Jesus stared down peacefully at her. From that time onward, the Iraqi woman felt and believed that she had received power to conceive children. Her womb was healed, and she gave birth to her firstborn son. Happily, other children followed.

JESUS HEALS ABUSED IRAQI WOMAN

We have met many abused women in the Middle East who have received comfort from the loving risen Savior! An Iraqi woman, Muna, is someone I know personally and I verify her story to be true:

> I was one of six daughters in Iraq. My father never loved me; he hated all of us sisters. He had always hoped that every daughter would be a boy. When he was told that we were girls, he called us goats.
>
> He never hugged or kissed me. I never heard from my father the words "I love you." We sisters and my Mother suffered much physical abuse from my father. Later I became a true believer in Jesus, whom I saw in dreams, and I wanted the joy of dancing in the Spirit as many Christian believers do, but my feet were frozen to the ground as if they were set in concrete. This is because of the hate-filled words of my father. He would enjoy Egyptian belly dancers on TV, but afterward he would say, "All of these women should have their legs broken." So I was afraid of expressing myself in worship by dancing in the Spirit. I could hear the words of my father that my legs should be broken!

Muna experienced a night vision of Jesus in which He gazed at her comfortingly and extended His hands to her in a gesture of invitation, warmth, and healing. But she was unable to reciprocate affection in the dream. The pain and inhibitions in her heart had been reinforced through the years of living under the roof of a tyrannical father.

Because Muna rejected the comforting advances of Jesus, in the dream He left her sorrowfully and walked past her down the stairs in her house in Baghdad. But she followed Him in the dream. She saw Jesus enter her father's room to hold an important discussion. Muna tentatively walked down the stairs in the dream and saw light streaming under the door. She heard Jesus rebuking and correcting her father's actions. Suddenly, Muna opened the door, and to her surprise, she saw a portrait of Jesus hanging on the wall as if He had become an honored family member. In the portrait, He resembled a Theophany of God the Father.

After this dream, Muna received the power to forgive her Father. She also received through the Spirit of God the ability to embrace an elderly, fatherly minister of the Gospel of Jesus Christ, and to be healed and delivered from an inordinate fear of the opposite sex. At a Gospel convention many years later in America, this Iraqi woman received the power from Jesus to dance reverently in the Spirit in public and to bring glory to the Heavenly Father. As led by the Holy Spirit, she was also empowered to weep with an Israeli Messianic brother as they forgave each other publicly for the hatred and bitterness that threaten to destroy their region.

BELIEVERS HAVE A "DIRECT LINE"

When normal methods of communication fail, we can still make contact with members of the Body of Christ via the Throne of God! During the most recent war in Iraq, it was not possible to write or to telephone our ministry contact in Baghdad. We did not know if he and his family were safe. But one night my ministry associate Shirley Hughes experienced a dream in which our Baghdad brother said, "Don't worry, Shirley. I am safe." Later we were able to reestablish contact with him through natural means, but in the Spirit world, contact had already been made through the reassuring dream.

JOURNAL OF SIGNS AND WONDERS

After much searching, through the hands of a pastor in the Galilee, we obtained a copy of a typewritten, mimeographed journal, *Signs and Wonders in Rabbath-Ammon, an Account of Divine Visitations in Amman, Trans-Jordan*, which was first printed in 1933. I also subsequently met upon three occasions with the remarkable niece of the prophetess involved in these extraordinary events, and my dear friend has verified the validity of the accounts and also printed the sheets into little pamphlets.

The prophet Amos in the Bible declared that the Lord will do nothing without first revealing his intentions to His servants, the prophets. That means that if the Church is listening to the Spirit of God, we will surely know things to come.

Through a series of signs and prophetic utterances, the Lord spoke in 1933 concerning the upheaval that would soon enfold the region. The Jordanian prophetess also predicted the return of the Jewish people. One of the most outstanding features of the phenomena was the speaking in recognizable languages unknown by the speaker, but in some cases understood by those who were listening, as on the Day of Pentecost.

Additionally, there were visible signs of a Dove "painted" in blood by a Hand from Heaven onto the forehead of the Christian woman, Hanneh Kawar. Pilgrims from all over Trans-Jordan witnessed these signs and traveled to hear her prophetic utterances that accompanied the signs.

The journal noted, *"Some word of explanation was probably needful of the salient features in the phenomena. This is all the more necessary as the fact of the supernatural in Christianity seems to have been overlooked, or to have been relegated to the bygone days of Apostolic Christianity or Hebrew history, if not altogether explained away by a rationalistic interpretation of Scripture.*

"If such a manifestation stands the test of Scripture, then it becomes a Divine Voice to a generation plunged in materialism and infidelity."

The reader was exhorted to note that the sign, which appeared on the forehead of the Arab Christian woman, was blood-like. Those familiar with the Holy Scriptures may recognize this significance. We quote one of the prophetic messages that explained the sign: "O foolish soul, I have wrought this sign that thou mightest understand that as there is no life without blood, so there is no salvation without blood." To this must be added the testimony of Scripture, Hebrews 9:22, "Without shedding of blood is no remission [of sins]." 1 John 1:7 also states, "The blood of Jesus Christ His Son cleanseth us from all sin."

Secondly, on the four occasions of the blood sign, it always took the shape of a dove. A prophetic message that accompanied the dove sign gave this interpretation: "The Spirit moveth around as a dove and settleth on the head of the true believer." Scripture says, speaking of Christ's anointing by the Spirit in Luke 3:22, "And the Holy Ghost descended in a bodily shape like a dove upon Him."

The sign of the Dove shaped in blood was therefore emblematic of the saving Blood of Jesus and the Holy Spirit as the seal of every true believer. Ephesians 1:13 states, *"In Whom also after that ye believed, ye were sealed with that Holy Spirit of promise."*

Furthermore, the sign on Hanneh Kawar's forehead was an antithesis of the soon-coming 666 mark of the Beast, the symbol of the antichrist described in the Book of Revelation. This Jordanian sign and wonder therefore recalled the sealing of God's servants on their foreheads in Ezekiel 9:4:

> *And the Lord said unto him, Go through the midst of the city, through the midst of Jerusalem, and set a mark upon the foreheads of the men that sigh and that cry for all the abominations that be done in the midst thereof.*

In my interviews with Mrs. Kawar's relative, I was told that the prophetess possessed a remarkable gift of the Word of Knowledge. Often the Holy Spirit would send Mrs. Kawar on a mission. She would be given the exact address of some soul who was in deep distress, and she would arrive on the scene just in time to bring a pertinent word from the Lord. A seasoned man of God who served a lifetime of Gospel preaching in Jordan was an eyewitness of the signs and also helped to document them.

Why a Woman as God's Instrument?

Some will naturally ask, especially in the male-oriented Middle East, if this sign and wonder was from Heaven, why was it placed upon a woman rather than a man? And why was a woman used to prophesy, especially as Arab society is overwhelmingly patriarchal? Perhaps the answer is found in Joel's great prophecy, which was quoted by the Apostle Peter in connection with the outpouring of the Spirit with signs and wonders on the Day of Pentecost: "And it shall come to pass in the last days, saith God, I will pour out of My Spirit upon all flesh: and your sons and your daughters shall prophesy" (Acts 2:17).

Female preachers are destined to be a peculiar characteristic of the endtime!

The Midnight Hour

One of the most outstanding and repetitive signs was that the phenomena often occurred at midnight. Was the Lord emphasizing the midnight hour when He will suddenly return as a thief in the night? The parable of the wise and foolish virgins climaxes with, "And at midnight there was a cry made, Behold, the bridegroom cometh!" (Matthew 25:6).

On the night of January 3, 1933, close to midnight, the Kawar family was amazed to discover blood on the mother's forehead resembling a dove with outstretched wings, covering her entire forehead but without touching her hair. When they asked what happened, the mother replied, "While I was asleep suddenly...there appeared a person clothed in light whose face shone as the sun, and He said in an audible voice: 'There shall come to pass great tribulation; fear ye not; the Lord is with you.'"

The family trembled and sensed a supernatural presence. As their hearts were filled with a wonderful joy, they praised God until 2:30 A.M., when curious neighbors arrived. Soon the news had spread and crowds of people came to see the sign. Fear and awe struck the faces of the majority, and they praised God for His work. Hundreds came to witness the sign until the next evening.

"On Thursday, the fifth of January," according to the elder son, "many crowds came and witnessed the blood, which remained absolutely clear, nor did we wipe it off, as we said that it had been placed by the Lord and should not be wiped off, for there might be a purpose in it. So it remained the whole of the sixth, but it became drier. A sister in charge of a hospital, an English lady, after examining the blood, said that she could not explain the presence of the blood in this form by any natural cause. A clergyman, who came especially, gave us his testimony that this event had a profound influence upon him. Many were profoundly stirred and resolved to repent and to lead a new and upright life."

A Voice Said, "Fear Not"

On another occasion at 2 A.M., the family was awakened again at the startled voice of Mrs. Kawar, who exclaimed, "While I was sleeping, suddenly I felt a hand pass over my forehead. Then I opened my eyes and clearly saw a hand removing the blood. At this I became afraid, when I heard a clear voice saying, 'Fear not.'"

On successive nights Mrs. Kawar began to sing in languages recognized to be German, French, Hebrew, and Greek. Here is one of the messages, which were always interpreted into Arabic (and the English translator of the journal put into "King James" style English):

- Rejoice and be glad O daughter of Zion for thy king cometh, Behold I come quickly. Behold ye are in the last days. For everything is accomplished, and all kindreds of the earth shall mourn over Him.

- And all believers are guarded in the everlasting arms.

- And all who have believed are saved, and all who have rejected Him will be punished forever.

- Ye shall behold the works of the Lord.

- Be zealous for the gifts.

- Be zealous for the work.

- Behold, I come quickly.

- Let not your faith be shaken.

- And all those who are prepared shall enter.

- And all the scoffers shall be cast out and the door shall be shut. Come, Lord Jesus.

Second Occurrence of Blood Sign

On the night of January 16 at about 4 A.M., Mrs. Kawar began to sing in the Spirit while asleep. Her daughter witnessed the blood appear quickly on her forehead from right to left, assuming the shape of a dove with outspread wings. All this took place while Mrs. Kawar was sleeping; she was not aware that the sign had been placed a second time.

The blood remained clear and plain to the sight for two days. Crowds thronged to witness the sign. Among these, an elder of the Evangelical Congregation in Es-Salt came to see the sign. He wiped a little of the blood with the end of his handkerchief, and the blood marked his handkerchief exactly as if ordinary blood had been wiped from the skin. About midnight, two nights later, Mrs. Kawar was conscious in her sleep that the same hand had removed the sign from her forehead.

On the night of January 25, Mrs. Kawar spoke this startling prophecy in light of the decline and perversity in the West:

- Were it not for my people I would have destroyed the inhabited earth.

- Woe, woe to those who have stood in the way of my people!

- The Lord knoweth them all.

- Kings pass away; all things pass away; and God the Judge abideth forever.

- Woe, woe to the world!

- Soon shall the cord be severed and the earth shall fall.

- The wicked taketh his pleasure and the poor dieth.

- The Spirit knoweth everything.

- God is beholding and the Judge is nigh.

- No one condemneth you [or, Let no one condemn you].

- My people shall return and all things shall be restored.

- Woe to those who stand in the way of My people!

- The Spirit of Truth bears witness.

- The North and the South shall meet; the True (or Truth) shall arbitrate; the Lord shall judge.

- The West shall be brought to an end [or, shall be perverse] and the East shall groan [or, The West is perverse and the East groaneth].

- "Woe to you, O perverse ones." The Lord shall judge.

Third Sign, A Standing Dove

At midnight on January 29, the family awoke to the sound of Mrs. Kawar's singing, while sleeping, and when they looked at her forehead, they saw the sign of blood in the shape of a standing dove placed upon her forehead.

Mrs. Kawar spoke various languages by the Spirit and translated the prophecies into Arabic:

- Everything the Spirit saith shall be accomplished.

- My people shall soon be gathered and shall come.

- Blessed be mine own [people]—every one of them.

- The Church shall be gathered and the tares removed.

- The Spirit of Truth [of the True One] witnesseth and shall accomplish [it].

- I will not be silent but will speak and my heart shall commune.

- Yea, yea, there shall be greater than this and many souls shall be added.

- How many men witnessed [saw] and have not borne witness!

- Every hard thing shall be solved by Him.

- I will go and meet the Spirit.

- Many shall speak by the Spirit and the dross shall be removed.

- Ye shall behold a great revival.

- And the little Zion shall be here [in Amman].

The preceding prophecy about a "little Zion" in Amman has given hope to many Jordanians to believe for revival. Indeed, it is prophesied that in the Last Days "the chief of the children of Ammon" shall escape out of the hand of the antichrist (Daniel 11:41).

After 4 A.M. the family was awakened to the sound of Mrs. Kawar's singing, and they saw that the sign had been completely removed.

Fourth Appearance of Dove Sign

There was a fourth appearance of the dove sign, and Mrs. Kawar spoke in the German tongue, interpreting in metrical Arabic the following hymn:

O ye sinners come to deliverance.

Rejoice and be glad in His word.

Crying, The Glory to thee we now shall give, Hallelujah.

Woe, woe to those who hinder the people from the way of salvation!

Warn, warn every one who cometh in touch with you.

There are three kinds of salvation: a sudden kind, a salvation by gradual stages, and a final salvation. [Three stages: justification, sanctification, redemption of body.]

Scoff not, O man, at the Spirit of God. Break and be humbled before the Creator.

Ponder, O believer, that thou shalt see with thine eyes the recompense of the wicked; and those who were scoffing at thee; so trust, and never be discouraged.

Rejoice, O thou who hast toiled for Me, and they whose soul has been abased, and they whose heart has been wearied; thou shalt wear a crown of glory and thy strength shall be manifested in a strange marvel.

During another three-month period, Mrs. Kawar received many long and beautiful prophecies of warnings of future hardships and exhortations to the Church. As these fiery words were circulated in pamphlets, a revival was stirred:

> "I chose many from amongst you, I chose many individuals. But ye have not obeyed My words. So I warn you now, I warn you again to return, to approach unto Me joyfully, and, lo, I will receive you. I will send forth of My Spirit upon you to arouse your dead consciences.... I separated you from the world, and ye have departed afar off; I separated you unto the ministry and ye paid no heed. Give ye now listening ears to the Spirit Who speaketh amongst you; give ye awe and reverence to God the possessor of the entire world.... I have now been of longsuffering patience toward you [literally in Arabic, I have prolonged My spirit] that ye might return unto Me, and ye have heeded not.

> "These are now the Last Days and I will pour out of My Spirit upon every one who hath returned unto me, and I will manifest wondrous works amongst you. Be glad and rejoice, O you whose hearts have cleaved unto Me, O ye who have loved, who have obeyed my commands. Show ye now love one to another as I have loved you to the end, unto death.... Israel shall soon return and the land shall be built up [or populated].

> "Despair thou not, neither grow thou faint, for I the Lord am thy keeper. Give thou glory to the Father and honor to the Son and reverence to the Holy Spirit.

> "Oft have I spoken in your midst and ye have heeded not, O ye of little faith. Hearken ye now unto My words and understand: behold I come shortly; Heaven and earth quiver with joy."

CHAPTER 8

Adventures Through Dreams

"We are such stuff
As dreams are made on and our little life
Is rounded with a sleep."
"The Tempest" (IV, I, 156-57) by William Shakespeare

Another famous Shakespearian line in Hamlet's soliloquy is "To sleep, perchance to dream."

Or, as I would put it, "Perchance to have an adventure through dreams!"

Since we spend a third of our lives sleeping, dreams can become a great adventure. When we sanctify our dreams before retiring to bed, calling upon the Lord to minister to us and binding satan from interfering, we can expect peaceful and revelatory rest.

The meaning and cause of dreams has fascinated scientists for centuries.

The brain is never idle, according to Professor Jim Horne in a May 2, 2006 article in Britain's *Daily Telegraph* newspaper. Professor Horne is director of the Sleep Research Centre at Loughborough University, and he notes that dreams "can be delightful and inspirational. Leonardo da Vinci attributed many of his inventions to them and wrote: 'Why does the eye see a thing more clearly in dreams than the imagination when awake?'"

However, Horne pointed out that in most cases it is "fairly clear that we dream as we think—dreams are a surreal pastiche of what we have recently encountered and thought about while awake. Why people want to place some meaning into dreams or interpret them is beyond the comprehension of many scientists, and probably those who write about the meaning of dreams. There is usually greater fantasy in the mind of the dream interpreter than the dream to be interpreted."

I would agree with the professor when it comes to the ordinary, run-of-the mill dream. However, as the Bible plainly teaches, God does invade our dreams from time to time to communicate with us. God especially states in his word that he will communicate with prophetic people in dreams (Numbers 12:6). So our dream experiences do need a good and sound Biblical interpretation.

In some cultures, the dream world is believed to be a place where a person's soul travels at night. In a sense, dreams confirm the soul's existence and the reality of another world. The Chinese believed that the soul leaves the body to visit this world, and if they should be suddenly awakened, their soul may fail to return to the body. For this reason, according to dream researchers, some Chinese today are wary of alarm clocks!

Native American tribes and Mexican civilizations also share the notion of a dream dimension. In the early nineteenth century, dreams were dismissed as stemming merely from anxiety or indigestion. Psychoanalyst Sigmund Freud revived and revolutionized the study and interpretation of dreams as significant signals of the subconscious mind. The Bible, on the other hand, refers hundreds of times to the importance of dreaming as one of God's most consistent methods of communicating to our spirits.

There are many types of dreams:

- *Residual Dreams.* These are ordinary dreams, the remainder of the day, that consist of information and symbols related to a person's recent or past experiences. This is like information processing or "replay" and is not necessarily prophetic or supernatural by definition.

- *Daydreams.* Daydreaming is classified as a level of consciousness between sleep and wakefulness when our imaginations are active. Everybody has a tendency to daydream. God can use them to inspire us to achieve great things as we meditate on his Word. However, daydreams can degenerate into undisciplined, ungodly thoughts, so it is wise to ask the Lord to fill our minds with godly thoughts.

- *Vivid "epic" dreams.* According to the Association for the Study of Dreams, laboratory studies reveal that we experience our most vivid dreams during a type of sleep called Rapid Eye Movement (REM). During REM sleep, the brain is very active, the eyes move back and forth rapidly under the lids, and the body's large muscles are unusually relaxed. REM sleep occurs every 90 to 100 minutes, three to four times a night, and lasts longer as the night progresses. The final REM period may span 45 minutes. This explains why vivid and memorable dreams seem to occur in the early morning hours. Since the Bible declares in Job 33:15 that the Lord speaks to us during "deep sleep," this would correspond to REM sleep. In Chapter 5, God spoke to Moussa during REM "deep sleep" when he reached a crisis of faith. Epic dreams are unforgettable and make a deep and lasting impression.

Some persons claim that they never dream, but according to scientists published on the Internet, these people simply do not remember their dreams. You may ask the Lord to help you retrieve important dreams from your memory banks, but a vivid epic dream will be sealed on your consciousness! During a long fast, I experienced an unforgettable vivid dream of God calling me to Israel; I am also unable to forget the details of my call to Arabia while in deep sleep.

- *Nightmare.* A frightening or disturbing dream that causes the dreamer to awaken abruptly feeling anxious and distressed. According to the Association for the Study of Dreams, nightmares are common among children between the ages of four and eight and fairly common among adults. Typical sources of nightmares are traumatic experiences, such as surgery or military combat, the loss of a loved one, a severe accident, an assault, medication, or illness. Upon awakening from a jolting nightmare, pray until your peace returns. Any attack deemed to be demonic should be rebuked instantly in the name of Jesus. Satanically inspired dreams are condemned in the Scriptures (see Deuteronomy 13:1-5). Diabolical dreaming is typical in pagan cultures where satan greatly influences the unconscious.

- *Common anxiety dreams* that occur across all cultures are chase scenes, taking examinations, and falling. It is superstitious to believe that a person will die if he falls and hits bottom in a dream. People have dreamed all kinds of horrors and have lived to tell the tale! The important thing is to pray after anxiety dreams and take authority over any anxious spirit or spirit of death.

- *Lucid dreams* occur when you realize you are dreaming in the middle of a dream! Most dreamers awaken themselves once they realize they are only dreaming. Other dreamers have cultivated the skill of remaining in the lucid state of dreaming. According to the Association for the Study of Dreams, *"lucid dreamers become an active participant in their dreams, make decisions in their dreams, and influence the dream's outcome without awakening."*

Therefore believers who are ruled by their spirits and not by their emotions should often dream lucid dreams. For example, if you are sexually violated or physically attacked in a defiling dream, the truly spiritual person will take authority over the attack *within the dream and will remain lucid*, because the spirit man never sleeps. When I have been embroiled in spiritual warfare, I have dreamed of being physically attacked. But within the dream I have taken authority in the name of Jesus against the perpetrator, and I have spoken a strong command within the dream for the attack to terminate. This control and awareness within lucid dreams can be likened to the operation of the Holy Spirit. Why? Because "the spirits of the prophets are subject to the prophets" (1 Corinthians 14:32)—even when we are dreaming. Our spirits never sleep although our bodies do. Therefore, if our spirits are strong in the Lord and in the power of His might, we will do exploits even in our dreams!

I was dreaming that I was walking down a road when a heckler followed me and became a nuisance. Suddenly I turned to him and commanded him to repent in the name of Jesus. He fell down on his knees and repented and suddenly many on the street were also repenting and praising the Lord. I enjoyed a revival in my dream because I deliberately took authority in the dream in the name of Jesus over the troublemaker.

- *Recurring Dreams.* God is visiting the Muslim people in supernatural recurring dreams, no doubt because of His mercy and because of His faithfulness to Abraham's seed. There have been many documented cases of Jesus personally appearing to Muslims, identifying Himself, and telling them they must believe and trust only in Him.

For example, Jesus appeared to an entire classroom of Muslim students where I subsequently visited the Arabian Peninsula under divine orders. I have also personally met two former Muslim Iranian girls, now Christian workers in their country, whose mother saw the Lord in a vision. Furthermore, I met a Muslim man during a Gospel event in Kano, Nigeria, who was introduced to Jesus in a dream.

Jesus took him by the hand and led him down a new road. The dream parable was a sign that the Nigerian must begin to walk with Jesus and become a Christian.

- *Intercessory Dream*. While researching dreams in the vast information available on the Internet, I read an article at earthpages.org entitled "The Dream: Teacher, Healer, Guide and Giver" by Michael W. Clarke. He mentioned a further category of dreams called "intercession" that struck a chord because such a dream is a very common occurrence for me:

"In the context of dreaming, intercession may or may not take place in real time. That is, one may dream of a negative situation which could take place in the future. In the dream state he or she mediates graces to another soul so as to engender healing or to encourage him or her to avoid making a negative choice.... One prays in a contemplative way for another within the context of the dream. As such, the ultimate source of healing or positive redirection is God, not the dreamer. Given the relativity of space-time, it's also conceivable that intercession dreams operate in real time and also with regard to past events."

- *"Macedonian Call."* This is a supernatural dream in which God directly imparts a commission to a person, usually giving directions to go somewhere. The Apostle Paul received a call to Macedonia in a night vision (Acts 16:9). A *man* in the dream asked Paul "to come over and help," but upon arrival, Paul didn't meet the man. Instead, Paul preached to a group of women at a river, then at Lydia's house. Next he delivered a demon-possessed woman, resulting in flogging and imprisonment. It seemed he was only reaching women. It wasn't until later that the Macedonian jailer from Philippi and his household were saved. Do you see that Paul fulfilled the vision progressively?

"MACEDONIAN CALLS" CONTINUE

Through a dream we also received a dramatic "Macedonian call" to the Philippines to stir revival to the Muslims.

It was a vivid, unforgettable dream in which a man in a long Filipino robe and Muslim-style hat was addressing a large audience. He yelled through the microphone, "Where are Christine and Peter Darg?" In the dream, we were sitting in the mid-section of a large congregation. I slid down in my seat. But the man called a second time very insistently, "Where are Christine and Peter Darg?" Slowly, I raised my hand. The man pointed dramatically to me and commanded very forcefully, "You must come to the north Philippines!"

When I awakened, I knew assuredly that God was definitely calling us to the North Philippines! It was a compelling dream, as are all "Macedonian call" dreams.

Contacts that previously had been eager for us to visit the Philippines were now strangely indifferent. When we booked the air tickets, we had no preaching engagements. Just a few days before we were to fly to Asia, no ministry engagements were confirmed.

What do you do in a situation like that? You must go on "Go!" It's enough that God is calling. Suppose we had not obeyed! What tremendous divine appointments and divine connections would have been forfeited!

Almost at the last minute, Nena, a wonderful sister at CBN Asia, coordinated a full ministry schedule, including media interviews. As we ministered, the Lord granted visions and prophetic words for the Philippines, and these revelations were broadcast on the national TV news! My interview was included on a top-rated secular TV show— and an actor was hired to dramatize my dream!

HEART CRY OF THE MUSLIMS

What was the dream's meaning? In the northern Philippine island where we landed, there were no people dressed like the man in the dream. But as I preached in the churches and asked questions, I learned that his style of clothing was typical garb of a southern Filipino Muslim, such as those who live on the island of Mindanao. The man's demanding call was simply the heart cry of the Muslims for the Gospel! He commanded us to come to the northern island because that's where the majority of the Christian workers live. The Holy Spirit led me to preach altar calls for evangelists to go to the Muslims, not only to their own countrymen, but also to the nations of the world.

I was told that nobody would respond to the altar calls because of fear of the Muslims. Nevertheless many dedicated believers rushed forward in every meeting, and some with travail and weeping, to offer their lives on the Gospel altar for the Muslims. A radio station began broadcasting to the Muslims as a result of one of those altar calls.

My husband Peter noted that the Philippine Islands were named after King Philip of Spain, whose namesake was Philip, the (flying!) evangelist of the New Testament. We prophesied: because of the Filipinos' knowledge of English and their ability to work "tent-making" jobs all over the globe, the mantle of world evangelism is falling upon that nation of islands.

I also saw the Gospel spreading like a fire in the Islamic south Philippines and a domino-like effect from East to West. Faithful Muslims in the Philippines have recently been experiencing dreams and visions of Jesus after Ramadan, the 30-day fasting month. These revelations were disclosed by a devout follower of "Isa" (Jesus) who works among the Tausugs, one of the biggest Muslim tribes in the islands. He relayed accounts of Muslims who met Jesus in their dreams. Reportedly they fasted extra days after Ramadan to receive special revelations from God concerning truth, according to the IsaalMasih.net Web site.

One resident of a remote village near Sinunuc could hardly believe that he had seen Isa (Jesus) defeating a giant dragon in sequential dreams! Another Muslim in the same district dreamed of Jesus healing many people. The following day, as he shared his dream, he told other Muslims that Jesus is the healer; he prayed for many, and they were all healed! The faith healer continues to profess that he is a Muslim, but he credits healing power to Jesus. The man reportedly says, "No one can save you but Jesus" when he prays for the sick. Pray for the discipling, theology, and doctrine of so many Muslims who are turning to Jesus through supernatural experiences!

Far-reaching Consequences

We thank God for our "Macedonian call" to the Philippines, for through that call we met the Kol Adonai Foundation whose leader subsequently moved to Jerusalem and established a ministry on the Mount of Olives, where I had already been preaching for years. Together we have, by the grace of God, established a large Gospel tent at the place where His feet shall be glorious on the Mount of Olives in anticipation and preparation for the Second Coming of Jesus! The Mount of Olives Gospel tent would not have unfolded in the fullness of time if God had not first sent us all the way to the Philippines through a dream!

Dreams Can Validate the Messenger

And they went forth, and preached every where, the Lord working with them, and confirming the word with signs following (Mark 16:20).

The Lord often prepares his chosen ones to receive his messengers. In the early part of this century, "Shaheeda," a Russian nurse, traveled throughout central Asia and Arabia as a Bible colporteur. She was welcomed into an Arab home for many seasons. The family accepted her teachings because the patriarch had previously seen her in a dream before she had ever entered his village. This phenomenon has also occurred in our ministry. Not only is it a great encouragement that I am in the right place at the right time, but validation in dreams also confirms the Gospel message that we preach! Such validation makes preaching very easy!

Once when I entered an Arab village, a family opened their home for a Gospel meeting because their son had dreamed that I would visit. Likewise, a *hajji* (a pilgrim to Mecca) prayed with me for salvation and healing because he had seen me in a dream.

When my husband and I were privileged to preach in eastern Bulgaria after the fall of Communism, two women testified that they had previously seen me in a dream. In a theater where we preached in Varna on the Black Sea, one of these women rushed forward at my Gospel invitation to receive Jesus. Just the night before, she had seen me in a vision: I caught her arm and saved her from falling into a deep pit! When she saw me preaching the following evening, she easily believed my message and came forward to repent and to receive Jesus publicly.

MINARET SUMMONS MUSLIMS TO THE GOSPEL

Two Bulgarian evangelists told me that the leader of a mosque in a village near Turkey's border had actually called the people to a Gospel meeting from the minaret! When I heard that staggering news, I jumped for joy and exclaimed, "Hallelujah! Truly these are the endtime when Muslims call their people from the minaret to hear the Gospel! Every tongue shall confess that Jesus is Lord—even the tongues of those who cry from the minarets five times a day!"

I was so overjoyed that the Bulgarian evangelists decided on the spot to organize an open-air campaign for me in the same region. With the help of a sound system, I preached to five thousand Muslim gypsies from a rooftop! That night many were saved and healed to the glory of God! A vision was fulfilled that I would preach to multitudes.

WARNINGS AND IRAQI ADVENTURE CONFIRMED IN DREAMS

Divine dreams also operate through my husband and myself as protective measures. Prior to different ministry trips into Turkey, as the group leader, I received warnings in night visions and dreams to change our team's strategies and itineraries. In one of the dreams, an intercessor who is a watchman for our ministry met me in an underground tunnel to alert me to change our itinerary. The message of the dream was clear and the interpretation of the underground tunnel meant to keep our plans hidden.

When we were called by the Lord to Iraq before the toppling of Saddam's regime, it was potentially a dangerous Gospel assignment. Who were we to obey—God or man? We sought the counsel of the trustees of our ministry and solicited much prayer from our ministry partners. But the Lord confirmed the assignment in a dream to my husband!

In a dream, my husband Peter saw me in a waiting room in one of Saddam Hussein's palaces. Saddam opened the door in a friendly manner and welcomed me into the country. This was a "Macedonian call," such as the Apostle Paul experienced, when in a dream he was led to a specific place. My husband Peter gave his blessing and felt assured my team would be safe. Although I had applied as "clergy" for an Iraqi visa, somehow the authorities listed me as "Minister of Religion." We were entertained as VIPs. The favor of the Lord followed us continually, and there was nothing concerning the Gospel assignment that we were prevented from accomplishing.

No Border Is Closed to Jesus

There are numerous reports of Jesus appearing in Islam's holiest city of Mecca, whose borders are closed to the Gospel—but they are not closed to the Holy Spirit! The Lord Jesus holds the keys to every city on earth. By the supernatural intervention of dreams and visions, the Lord is having mercy on whom He will have mercy.

A pilgrim Muslim was circling the Ka'aba Stone, Mecca's holiest site, when Jesus appeared to him in a white robe. Many such accounts exist! Jesus said to the pilgrim, "I am the Way, the Truth, and the Resurrection Life. Believe on Me." Then Jesus disappeared in the throng.

The Mystery of the Saudi Bus Driver

A similar, highly fascinating incident is recounted in Jane Rumph's book, *Stories from the Front Lines*[1]. An Indonesian *imam* (mosque leader) from the island of Sumatra made the *hajj* (pilgrimage) to Saudi Arabia. The journey was truly the spiritual turning point of his life, but not in the way he had expected. He was seeking a religious experience from Allah, but never imagined he would receive revelation from a bus driver.

While on a bus tour of outlying holy sites, the Indonesian imam was sitting up front and listened for hours to the driver preach to him about Jesus! The imam's heart burned within him as he listened to the bus driver. One of the things the driver emphasized was that God wanted a personal relationship with the imam and not just religious ritual from a distance...and Islam could never offer that.

To the pilgrim's surprise, the driver disappeared after one of the excursions, and was replaced by another. Upon return to his home country, the imam visited a Chinese Christian neighbor. He was shocked to discover a picture of the Saudi bus driver on the wall of his Chinese friend's home—it was an artist's depiction of Jesus!

APOCALYPTIC DREAM AND MY ARABIAN NIGHT

While preaching in Florida, one night I experienced an awesome apocalyptic dream. God's cry for evangelism was at stake. I saw a Middle Eastern person under divine judgment, heavily chained, fearful, and ready to be executed. A molten monolith of gold falling from Heaven, symbolic of God's judgment, would soon obliterate this forlorn soul. But the gigantic bar fell short with a terrible crash, and the execution was mercifully stayed. As I awakened, the Holy Spirit said, "There is yet time to win the lost."

When the Holy Spirit imparts a message in a dream, we must be careful to discover and interpret all He has in mind. One night when I was visiting California, I experienced a dream in which I saw the map of the Arabian Peninsula. A shaft of light pointed straight as an arrow to a certain city named on the map, and I heard the voice of the Holy Spirit exclaim very authoritatively, "Go!" As a result of this dream, I often teach that when God speaks to us, his choice of words can be very economical.

In my mind, when I awakened, I did not think that the name of that particular city I had seen in my dream was correct, because I had mistakenly confused its name and geographical location with Djibouti, a nation on the horn of East Africa.

The following day, I flew to minister at a conference in Nashville, Tennessee, where I asked the Lord for a confirmation of the previous night's dream. At an intercessor's house, a group of intercessors began to pray, and a woman began to prophesy. Instantly, I sensed a knowing in my spirit that her prophecy would be a confirmation of my call to Arabia!

She said, "I see a beautiful boot, but it is inappropriately bound with old shoelaces." Somebody in the group added a spontaneous word of knowledge, "This boot is not Italy, but Arabia! And the Arabian boot is inappropriately bound! God is sending you to loose the boot!"

The intercessor owned a large world map that she kept in her bedroom for frequent prayers. We rushed to the room and found the map. We were stunned to see that the Arabian Peninsula is shaped like a boot. I had never noticed that before. And the place where the boot-laces should be prophetically untied was positioned exactly where the Holy Spirit had commanded me to go in the dream. Indeed, the city I had seen in the dream was exactly where it was supposed to be on the map on the Arabian Peninsula!

A SECOND CONFIRMATION ABOUT ARABIA IN A DREAM

In a second dream, I saw the Arabian "boot" arise from the map and dance a jig of joy on North Africa with a liberty that comes from knowing the way of salvation. This dream told me that Arabia will be set free to serve the living Savior. Joy shall come to Islamic North Africa as well!

The Holy Spirit is returning to that which was in the beginning as the program of evangelization amongst the Gentile nations is coming full circle and to a conclusion.

Oh, how our Lord answers prayer! We would be far more diligent to pray and to prophesy if only we could see through the veil the eternal answers that are wrought by our prayers!

PRAYER, SIGNS, AND WONDERS SIMULTANEOUSLY COORDINATED

At the beginning of the Muslim fast of Ramadan, in Jerusalem on February 19, 1994, we began to intercede fervently in the Spirit for that Arabian city where the Holy Spirit had commanded me to go, but I had not yet received a release of finances to travel there. I and two others, (including my prophetic intercessor Ali, described in Chapter 2), were praying at our ministry center on the Mount of Olives. Ali saw a vision of doves being released all over the Arabian Peninsula as we prayed.

Simultaneously, on February 19, 1994, Jesus appeared in the city of the prayer target. Yes, He appeared in the exact city that I had seen on the map! He manifested His glory not just to one person, but to an entire classroom of ten-year-old Muslim boys! It is wonderful when Jesus manifests his presence to just one person, but when He appears to an entire group, to 21 young boys at once, that is an outstanding and undeniable miracle! For the Bible says, "at the mouth of two witnesses, or at the mouth of three witnesses, shall the matter be established" (Deuteronomy 19:15).

> *Not unto us, O Lord, not unto us, but unto thy name give glory, for thy mercy, and for thy truth's sake. Wherefore should the heathen say, Where is now their God? But our God is in the heavens: he hath done whatsoever he hath pleased* (Psalm 115:1-3).

In the providence of God, finances were released to us and we met the students, their lovely principal, and the teachers—all for whom we had apparently been interceding!

They testified that a bright light had entered the schoolroom, and the Lord Jesus appeared in a white Arab-style robe with a green mantle. The children were surprised that the visitor carried the Holy Bible, since they were familiar only with the Koran. As Jesus blessed each of the boys, *He appeared to be One person and yet Three persons.*

Revival fire fell in the school as a result of this open vision! The revival atmosphere resembled accounts of some of the world's best-known revivals. For example, in the Scottish Hebridean revival, people fell down in the streets under the power of God—not just in church buildings. It was the same in this Arabian revival. When some Muslims walked onto the school compound, they fell down under the power of God. They were pinned down by the *kavod* (weight) of the Holy Spirit for 45 minutes. They had no knowledge or intention of attending a revival! They unknowingly ventured into the vicinity, and they were struck down by the power of God. And when they were finally able to stand, they requested *Bibles!*

ENDNOTE

1. Jane Rumph, *Stories from the Front Lines,* (Longwood, FL: Xulon Press 2001).

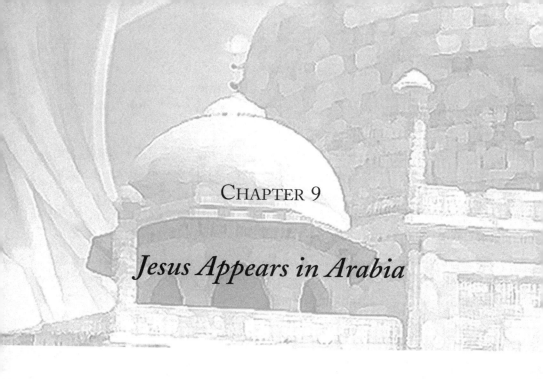

CHAPTER 9

Jesus Appears in Arabia

What is so staggering to me personally is that we were praying for the city of the Lord's visitation in an anointed prayer meeting on the Mount of Olives in Jerusalem on February 19, 1994, the very day of the dramatic visitation! Because God had commanded me in a dream with the simple word "Go" to visit that city, we were praying fervently for the finances to travel when the Arabian visitation occurred.

My prayer partners and I were crying for the spirit of salvation to be released in that city. I did not know about our connection with these occurrences until my husband and I visited the city by faith, knowing nobody, except the Holy Spirit. But He is more than enough. When you know the Holy Spirit and are sent by Him, you hold the key to any city on earth.

The story behind the finances for the mission is also worthy of note. One day, while I was standing on a subway platform, a word of knowledge just dropped into my spirit that Muslim money would pay for many of our Gospel campaigns. Subsequently, an American businessman felt led to finance our Gospel Meetings in India—and so we routed a stopover visit to the Arabian city I had seen in my dream. The businessman's wife told me that the funds came from transactions with Arabs living in the very city I had seen in the dream! Only God could have coordinated everything behind the scenes!

Upon our arrival in that Arabian city, my husband and I asked some Indian expatriate believers, "Where is the Holy Spirit moving here?" They told us about the visitation of the Lord at a school administered by an Indian Christian lady, so we went there and became a part of that revival, preaching and praying for the sick.

In the New Testament the risen Lord Jesus appeared to many of the disciples simultaneously, and at another time, "he was seen of above five hundred brethren at once" (1 Corinthians 15:6). However, throughout the history of the Church corporate gatherings that have witnessed a bodily vision of the resurrected Jesus have been rarely reported. The fact that He appeared to an entire classroom of twenty-one Muslims is one reason why the visitation in Arabia is especially outstanding, and it is also significant to current events.

I believe the extraordinary visitation and revival were a result of at least four factors:

- the Lord's timing to reach Arabia in answer to Abraham's prayer;
- because of the boys' own hunger for God;
- because of the administrator's hunger for more of Jesus. The school's founder, Mrs. George, told me that prior to the Visitation she had been crying out to God almost continually to see the face of Jesus;
- because of our own intercessions in Jerusalem, by the grace of God.

Fascinating testimonies of the Muslim children and how the Lord appeared to each of them simultaneously in the 1994 Arabian visitation have been carefully documented by the school below. These children whose parents were expatriates represented many Muslim nations.

A Day I Will Never Forget
By M. Sulman from Dar Es Salaam, Tanzania

February 19, 1994 was the most wonderful day of my life. I was praying in the morning and I saw a gentleman just up in the sky. I got shocked, but when he came closer to the ground, I saw him becoming three men, and I couldn't understand which was the real man. He just entered the classroom's window like a ghost. I was nearly about to faint, but in this man there was something different. When he saw me, he was smiling. Then he was coming nearer and nearer. First I got scared so much, but this time my heart was not beating fast. It was filled with happiness. As he was walking the same thing happened—he was becoming three and again becoming one, again three and again one.

Now I saw that he was holding a very old book in his hand. It had "H.B. King James Magnificent" on it. This time was the most important time when he came and stood near me. I was very, very, very scared. But when I felt his soft hand touch across my head, it was like as if pure Heaven waters was running across my body.

Then he asked me for my wishes. First I thought of games and play and to enjoy the life. Then I thought once more. The final exam was coming closer. Then I told him my wishes without fear, that I wanted to pass the final exam. He touched my head and said, "It is done." I didn't want to blink my eyes even for a second because he was so beautiful that I wanted to look and look and look at him.

But my teacher could not see him. We told her he was touching her head, but she did not know it. Later I passed the exam. Now when I am not scared of this man, he no more comes to see me but only visits me in my prayer and dreams. If I need something he gives it to me. I will never forget him in my life.

My Very Strange Experience
By M. Zakin from Zaire

The date in which this strange thing happened was on 19.2.94. I saw a shot of golden light coming towards us. It became more and more bigger. At last I saw that it became a streak of light, and it came in the class and dashed on the walls. Then it came behind the class. Just then a man appeared with a long white dress. It was something like a kandura and had a green cloth on one side. He even wore old sandals. He was so tall that he almost touched the ceiling. He looked very handsome. He was very fair and had curly hair. He brought a book with letters H.B. He wore a golden bangle on his head. He was very beautiful. He went around the class and touched everybody's head. When he came near me, I got a nice smell of rose flowers. Teacher was very angry with our class because we made much noise. She did not see him, but we all saw him touch her on her head. When I went home I was thinking and thinking about this. I felt like fever. My parents asked me what had happened and I told them. They too didn't believe me, like teacher. They took me to the mosque and we met the mullah. I told him everything. He said that *Issa Nabie* [Jesus the Prophet] had visited us, and it is for good. So we were all happy. I know you feel it is hard to believe it, but whatever I saw is very true. He gave me all my wishes. He said, "It is done." I often think about this strange experience.

An Unforgettable Experience
By I. Iqbal and I. Rashid from Sudan

It was 19th February 1994. We were praying usually, when something happened. We could see the window, and to our surprise we saw black clouds. Then a moment later a streak of light just passed through the window. It bounced off a wall and landed at the back of the class. We were astonished to see a man at the back of the class. He was a very tall man almost reaching to the top of the ceiling. He had fair, brown curly hair and was wearing a long white dress with a green cloth. He was wearing old worn-out sandals with a big golden ring on top of his head. He was so strange but so handsome. He had in his hand one old leather book with H.B. letters. He went around and touched everyone's head. Our teacher entered the class and he touched her head also. The teacher was angry with us because we shouted, "Teacher, the man is touching you!" She did not know anything that was going on. As the prayer finished he disappeared.

A Thrilling Experience in My School Life
By M. Farook from Egypt

I was praying in class on 19 February 1994. It was a beautiful day and suddenly dark clouds appeared in the sky, and a streak of light came through the window and bounced on the walls several times and stopped. And I saw a man, very tall, touching the ceiling. He was very fair with brown curly hair touching his shoulders. He was wearing a white kandura with a green cloth. He was carrying an old book with a golden border with something like H.B. written on it. I saw a bangle on his head and he asked us for three wishes. I told him my wish. I wanted to become first or second in the class. But I became fourth. I felt cold water running through my heart when he touched me. He touched teacher, but she did not feel it. He disappeared as we finished the prayer.

A Day I Cannot Forget
By Ibne from Morocco

We were praying in a classroom on 19th February. Our window was black. Actually, outside the window there were some black clouds. Then a streak of light dashed on the wall and because of that streak of light we could not see what it was. A boy in our class became momentarily blind. A man appeared from the streak of light. He was a tall man almost touching the ceiling. He was fair with brown curly hair. He wore a long white dress with a green cloth and old sandals. He had an old leather book with a gold border. H.B. was written on it. He went around touching our heads and asked for three wishes. I felt like cold water was flowing through my heart. We told our wishes. The man had a golden light on his head. He was looking very nice. I felt like I was in the air. He granted my wishes. He touched Teacher also. Teacher said she didn't know what we were saying to her. The man disappeared. Suddenly after the prayer finished, the boy who could not see could now see. This day is a very strange day that I will never forget.

A Strange Day
By Amin from Egypt

We were praying in the morning on 19th February 1994. Then we saw dark clouds outside the window. Then it bounced on the window very slowly and then it stood at the back of the class. We were still praying. My friend could not see him and another could not talk. Then one friend turned back to see that everyone was praying. Then he saw three men becoming one. He came in front slowly and he touched everyone's head and said, "What are the three wishes you want?" First I asked him for video games and then I asked him to make me pass in the exam that was coming near. I got a higher position in the class for the first time. He wore a kandura and his hair was brown and curly and it reached to the shoulder level. He had a round golden bangle and he held the Holy Bible. He went and golden footsteps were on the ground. Then our prayer finished and he disappeared. I told my parents, but they did not believe me at first, but after some time they said, "It's a miracle."

The Memorable Day of My Life
By M. Shoboh from Tanzania

It was 19th February 1994. We were praying. Suddenly outside there was a black cloud with thunder. Then a streak of light and it just passed through the window. The streak hit the walls at the back of the classroom and it appeared to get the form of a man. Each and every step he took there below on the ground were silver sandal prints. He was very tall with curly hair. He wore a kandura and a green shawl. He looked very handsome. I felt as if he was a stranger. His sandals were worn out. I closed my eyes in terror. Suddenly when I opened my eyes I saw him near me. I was very afraid. My friend and I were leading the prayer. He had an old leather book with a gold border. He had a bangle above his head. Suddenly he touched me and asked me for three wishes. I saw him touching teacher and my friend, but only my friend saw him. Teacher could not see him or feel him. That time we were singing the song, "I am blessed." From this day started my luck.

The Visit (A Memorable Day)
By Rasool from the Sudan

In the morning of February 19th, 1994, during the morning prayer, I had a strange experience. I had prayed once before with my friends, but that morning when I was praying with my friends at 8:15 A.M., I heard someone talking to me. I could not open my eyes, but I felt strange. I knew someone big was standing very close to me. I could feel it. He urged me to say in my prayer what I needed. At first I thought, "Who is this guy, what does he want?" But he had a strong voice and I obeyed. As I had asked, a day later, my brother was born and in that trimester exam (III Trimester), I got the first place. My friends said that they saw him. They also said to me that he talked to almost everyone. The visitor was different from all others. Something was special about him. I felt so very happy. It was a memorable day, and I can't forget this incident, most of all the visitor, because my wishes were said in the prayer and they came true. I think he is a saint.

The Day I Cannot Forget
By Ahmed from Somalia

That was the most wonderful day in my life. We were praying on 19.2.94. I saw dark clouds outside the window. Suddenly I saw a streak of light enter our class through our window. The streak of light passed through the eyes of my friend. The streak hit the blackboard and went at the back of the class. I was the first one to see him. I was too afraid and turned my face away. My friend tried to ask me what I was doing, but I couldn't answer. The stranger was very handsome and tall. He had a white robe and a green coat over him and had a gold circle on his head. He had a book, which was old, and asked our wishes. He said our wishes were granted. Even he touched our teacher's head and asked her wishes. When he touched mine, I felt cold water flowing through my heart. Each step he took there was a golden light on the floor. After we finished our prayer we couldn't find him. I wish to see him again.

A Day I Will Never Forget
By S. Falah from Dar Es Salaam

Our class was praying during the month of February. It was Ramadan. The date was 19th. Soon we saw dark clouds and from the window a flash of light came and banged the wall. A man appeared from the clouds. The man was tall—touching the ceiling—and he was fair. He had curly hair. The colour of his hair was brown. He had a piece of green cloth on his shoulder. He was wearing a white kandura. He kept an old book in his hand. It had a leather cover with a gold border with H.B. and there was also a King's name on it. A golden bangle was on his head. He was handsome and beautiful. He came around and asked us three wishes. I felt like ice water falling on me when he touched me. There was a flower smell in the class. I told him my wishes and it was granted. I told him to bless my parents, brothers, and friends. He touched our teacher. We shouted, "Teacher, the man is touching you," but she asked, "What man?" She didn't see him. After the prayer was finished we didn't see him.

Comments on the Manifestation Of Our
Lord Jesus Christ on February 19, 1994
By Mrs. George, Headmistress

This book contains the details of a very powerful and mighty vision. This vision has opened in a keen way the inward eye of our faith, that is the faith of more than a hundred teachers who are working in an institution brooded over by God's glory in a city of the Arabian Peninsula. It has now led to a new ministry, VIVIT, VIVIT (which in Latin means, "HE IS ALIVE! HE IS ALIVE!").

Yes, now we are excited! For deep down in our heart, our faith is firmly rooted, and we now know for sure that the mighty name of Jesus is not a mere name in history. He is not the man that was. Jesus is not just the landmark of time, as history is referred to Him by the use of A.D. (Anno Domini) or B.C. (Before Christ), but He is the God that WAS, that is, and that WILL BE. He is alive. Yes, He rose from the dead and His mighty presence is with us, so close that we can hear His heartbeat of abundant love and concern. We can sense His love and feel the warm vibration of His eternal love.

We teachers are all touched by the power of this mighty vision, so blessedly given unto twenty-one innocent ten-year-old Muslim children. Ever since, our lives have been changed. We no longer mess our lives with the temporary passing desires of this world: WE WANT, WE DESIRE, WE THIRST now only for one thing in our life—OUR Lord. We seek Him continuously and we read the Bible, the Holy Book we teachers knew from our childhood.

But now it gives a new vision, a new anointing, and a new wisdom to know Him better, to love Him better, and to serve Him better. We want to avoid all sinful habits, for we dare not grieve our divine Holy Lord. We do not want to be separated from Him, for now we know the danger of this separation causes oppression by the evil one.

Has Jesus been the man of the past, as history declares? Is the Bible you have seen all your life just like any other book you have seen and read? No! No, dear friend. If this divine vision that appeared in our school has changed so positively our lives, your faith can also grow, and you shall spread as the mighty branches of the true vine that Jesus is.

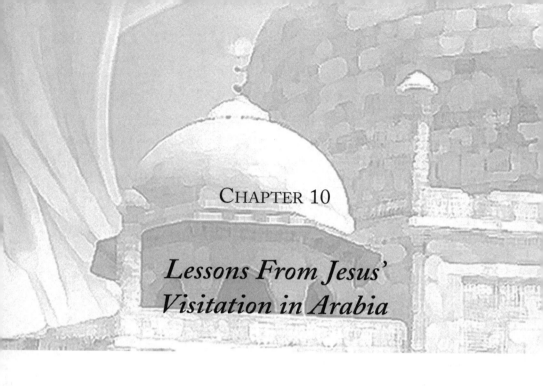

CHAPTER 10

Lessons From Jesus' Visitation in Arabia

Jesus "...showed Himself alive..." (Acts 1:3).

The following song was composed by a ten-year-old Muslim boy named M. Sulman and was taught to his fellow classmates. It was this cry for God that the children were singing when Jesus appeared simultaneously to them, showering them with His presence, love, and mercy:

I Am Blessed

I am blessed, I am blessed
Every day of my life I am blessed.
When I wake up in the morning
And as I lay my head to rest,
I am blessed, I am blessed.
More of you, more of you
Thirsty I cry, God hear my cry
I need more of you.

As the boys stood singing the beautiful words, "More of you…thirsty I cry" on a February morning during Ramadan, the Savior of the World entered the school to answer that cry.

The large window of the corner classroom gently wafted with clouds, and then brilliant golden rays penetrated and finally shaped into the "beautiful," "strange," "gentleman," "special" "person." He held an "old book" with golden edges. They saw that the book was embossed with "HB," standing for Holy Bible. Jesus is the Word, and the Word is Him. (It is fascinating that more than one of these Muslim boys noted that Jesus was carrying a King James Version of the Holy Bible! It is not likely that these Muslim children could have known about theological debates over various translations, but this vision gives credence to those who think that the King James Version is "heaven's" choice!)

> *And the Word was made flesh, and dwelt among us, (and we beheld his glory, the glory as of the only begotten of the Father,) full of grace and truth* (John 1:14).

Jesus stood there radiant before the children, gloriously combining the Word, the Bible, and His presence, as a parable of Who He is—the Word of God!

It is notable that the headmistress, Sister George, had been crying out to God for many months before the visitation occurred. She was a born-again believer, but she was desperate in her heart for personal revival, to know more of the power of God. Her constant prayer had been, "Jesus, let me see your face!" Her prayer was answered beyond her wildest imaginations, when the Lord showed His face to her Muslim pupils!

"Now," say the teachers, "we know the Word (Holy Bible) is the only way to know Him."

The Principal also cried, "How often have we not hesitated to sacrifice thousands of dollars to enter a university to seek worldly knowledge through the books of this perishing world while the most precious Book of Life lies ignored in some corner of your home?

Parents, how many of you are now ready to give this divine wisdom to your children? Please turn aside and cast a simple glance at your Islamic brother. Literate or illiterate he may be, but his holy book has a special place in his house. The family members approach that book with reverence. They are taught the Koran from a very early age. Dear Christian brother, while the truth is locked in your chest, have you ever exposed the truth of your Holy Bible to your child with the same reverence? Does the Word of God have a special place in your home and in your heart? Are your children disobedient? Are they with the world and its wayward ways of drugs, drunkenness, lust, and evil desires? Wake up! For the Word shall shape your child at a very tender age. Then your dreams regarding your child will become realized."

Mrs. George continued her exhortation: "Remember now thy Creator in the days of thy youth, while the evil days come not, nor the years draw nigh, when thou shalt say, 'I have no pleasure in them.' (Ecclesiastes 12:1) For if your child has known his Creator from the days of his youth, through the Word, he shall stand firm and bring blessing into your household."

HIS GARMENTS

Jesus was stripped of His garments when He was made sin in our stead on the Cross. But after His death, burial, and ascension, He is always appropriately arrayed in glorious garments. John envisioned Jesus clothed with a robe down to the feet (Revelation 1:13).

The students called the visitor's garment a white "kandura" (robe). The boys also saw a green mantle, which is a heavenly reflection of the emerald rainbow that encircles the Throne of God (Revelation 4:3). (This revelation was especially fascinating to me, since the heavenly vision I had received as a child was the compassionate healing Jesus wearing a white robe with green stripes, perhaps also reflective of the emerald rainbow circling God's throne!)

In the Old Testament, the High Priest wore a diadem of pure gold (Exodus 28:36-38). Jesus being the Heavenly High Priest wore fittingly, in the words of the children, "a golden bangle on his head."

THE TRIUNITY OF GOD

The Triunity of God could not have been better explained by theologians than through this simple vision and the boys who declared, "I saw him as three; I did not know which of the three He was, but I saw him again as one." Praise be to the Father, to the Son, and to the Holy Spirit, One True God who manifests in Three Persons.

THE OMNIPRESENCE OF GOD

The vision had lasted only a few minutes, but during that very short time, each boy felt that the Lord was personally beside him, touching him. "When He touched me, I felt like [I was] being washed with cold water," says the child. All the children, simultaneously saw, heard, and felt the close proximity of His divine presence. The Lord is omnipresent, here, there, and everywhere, all around your home, in your country and in all the countries of this planet, and in every nook of this universe. The mighty omnipresence of our omnipotent, omniscient Lord is awesome.

> *Prayer*: Lord and Master, how well you have taught us your divine omnipresence through this wondrous vision. We adore you, Jesus. Thank you that you promised never to leave us nor forsake us!

A REAL PERSON

Our Lord Jesus is not some disembodied spirit, spread out, vague, and formless, but He is very much a person. By all these little children, He was seen in the vision as a person, a concerned person, and a practical, loving friend asking them what they needed. To their expressed desires He simply said, "It is done." His loving, beautiful, and awesome presence, beyond description, with a golden, radiant light around His head, yet with worn sandals on His divine feet, represented a more simple form of a man. But as He walked around the class, wherever His divine feet moved, there were sparks of silver and gold. The old sandals remind us that Jesus is from the dateless past to the present and to the endless future as the great I AM. If His feet now walk on streets of gold, it is not surprising that his footprints were golden and full of light!

Fragrance and Living Waters in a Dry Land

Our Lord is the "rose of Sharon" (Song of Songs 2:1); His name is as "ointment poured forth" (Song of Songs 1:3); and "all your robes are fragrant" (Psalm 45:8). More than one of the children reported that His presence brought the fragrance of "roses" or "flowers." His Word also washes us clean. Many recalled the sensation of cold water flowing through their hearts. This is very relevant for the dry, Arabian Peninsula and is surely a sign of our Lord who gives "living waters" to all who are thirsty. Jesus said, "Whosoever drinketh of the water that I shall give him shall never thirst; but the water that I shall give him shall be in him a well of water springing up into everlasting life" (John 4:14).

A Parable in Demonstration

Another important lesson from the Arabian visitation is an exemplification of Matthew 18:3. Jesus said, "Verily I say unto you, Except ye be converted, and become as little children, ye shall not enter into the kingdom of Heaven." It must be carefully noted that while the children collectively saw the vision, the teacher (though very much present) had no idea what was happening! The boys did not know who "the Man" was, and so they cried aloud, "Teacher, the Man is touching you!" She did not see Him, nor did she hear Him! This valuable part of the visitation is a parable of a very important truth: As we pray, His presence is so close to us. But even as He touches us, we like this teacher, are not always receptive. In our hardened adult ways, we sadly often do not sense His mighty, beautiful presence and touch.

But if we humble ourselves and become like tenderhearted children, we too shall have our spiritual senses opened to hear Him and to see Him face-to-face!

> *Prayer of Consecration*: Dear Heavenly and Merciful Father, in Jesus' name I come to You. Take me as I am and make me what I ought to be in spirit, in soul, in body. I acknowledge

my sins and turn from them. I humble myself as a little child to put my faith right now in the living Lord Jesus as my only Savior. I thank you and believe that He died for my sins and that He was declared to be the Son of God with power by the resurrection from the dead! Come, Holy Spirit, and live in me and guide me always. Give me power to do right. I confess with my mouth that Jesus is my Lord. If I have wronged anyone, help me make restitution. No matter what it costs, wash me now in the Blood of Jesus that I may become Your child forever and manifest You in a perfect spirit, a holy mind and a healthy body. In Jesus' name, Amen and Amen!

CHAPTER 11

More Signs, Wonders, and Miracles

To summarize so far, we have established the importance of dreams and visions, not based upon subjective feelings, but upon the revealed methods of God.

The Lord declared in the Old Testament that he would speak through dreams and visions, and he reiterated the promise in the New Testament (Joel 2:28; Acts 2:17). Additionally, God declared in the Old Testament, "If there be a prophet among you, I the Lord will make Myself known unto him in a vision, and will speak unto him in a dream" (Numbers 12:6). And in Hosea 12:10, God testifies concerning Himself, "I have also spoken by the prophets, and I have multiplied visions, and used similitudes, by the ministry of the prophets."

Furthermore, the Psalmist assures us that the Lord will give counsel in the nighttime: "I will bless the Lord, Who hath given me counsel: my reins also instruct me in the night seasons" (Psalm 16:7). The realms of visions and dreams open to us the possibility of receiving not only guidance and revelation from God, but also gifts of the Spirit and healings. King Solomon received the gift of wisdom in a dream, while

Abram, on the other hand, received an extremely important covenant during deep sleep: "And when the sun was going down, a deep sleep fell upon Abram.... In the same day the Lord made a covenant with Abram" (Genesis 15:12-18).

However, having established the Biblical validity of dreams and visions, we must continue to emphasize that the work of salvation—Jesus Christ saving the eternal soul of a person—is just as great a miracle or sign and wonder as an open vision or a leaping cripple. The transformation of the inner person is even more significant than any physical or supernatural sign.

Listed among the "power gifts" in 1 Corinthians 12 are the gifts (*charismata*) of healing as well as the working (*energema* = energy, operation) of miracles (*dunamis* = power). We tend to call healings "miracles" when most are just that—healings—whereas the working of miracles is a separate operation of the Spirit. The word for miracles is *dunamis* (Strong's 1411), meaning "miraculous power," sometimes translated as "mighty deeds." St. Thomas Aquinas rightly claimed that to be a miracle, an event had to be beyond the natural power of any created thing to produce.

Dreams and visions should characterize the Spirit-filled life. This is the time of the revival of exploits, of mighty works, characterized by acts similar to those accomplished by Biblical heroes. The Church desperately needs the supernatural, especially since Jesus Himself prophesied in Matthew 24:24 that in the Last Days false christs and false prophets will demonstrate "*great* signs and wonders" (emphasis mine).

Satan will increasingly promote lying wonders and falsehoods. Therefore the discerning of spirits should be one of the most coveted gifts of the Spirit so that the believer can expose satan's pseudo-wonders, a special characteristic of the endtime. We should petition the Lord for greater discernment and for genuine miracles from God.

Our generation has witnessed not only the restoration of the healing gifts but also the working of miracles, visions, and dreams, particularly in the Holy Land. Even though God is the source of miracles,

He still uses agents. Elderly Sarah birthed a baby; Moses' rod worked miracles; Aaron's rod flowered; Balaam's donkey spoke; Elijah controlled the elements; Elisha's bones resurrected the dead; Jesus fed 5,000 and raised Lazarus; Peter and Paul executed divine judgments, causing many to fear and reverence God; and Peter's shadow healed the sick.

The early Church Fathers also looked upon miracles as signs. St. Augustine wrote a treatise on the importance of dreams. The Anglo-Saxon saint Cuthbert was compared to the Apostles because miracles confirmed his preaching. St. Martin was linked with the miracles of Christ, particularly the ability to raise the dead. The sixth-century monk St. Maur was reputed to have walked on water like Jesus. And miracles have continued through the ages right up to our time.

After his conversion to Christ through a vision, the Indian saint Sundar Singh renounced Sikhism and was poisoned by his family, but he survived, to their utter amazement, and became well known for his Christ-like character. He was born in 1889 but disappeared in the foothills of the Himalayas in 1929—many people believed he was raptured to Heaven and several books have been written about his life; details are readily accessible on the Internet.

The extraordinary is possible if we will expect to move in the miracle realm. Expectation is part of the process to trigger the working of miracles, to believe to hear messages from God in visions, and to see "love letters" from the Lord in dreams. The saints of all ages have believed that miracles are authenticating signs from God to show his approval of Gospel preaching.

After being soaked in winter flash floods during our Gospel outreach to the Palestinian village of Nablus, neither our clothes nor our shoes remained wet. This miracle of traveling through the wet weather dry-shod was a sign that God endorsed our plans and the distribution of many Gospels (*Injils*) to Muslims in the West Bank of Biblical Judea and Samaria. Accompanying me were Shirley Barley and evangelist Dahood. My Jerusalem pastor had blessed our going, although he did acknowledge the danger of it—but I had "seen" that we should go to Nablus. The rain had washed away any troublemakers, and when we reached the town square the sun came out. We distributed every one of our Bibles within ten minutes.

Somebody wrote to me, "Sister Christine, the so-and-so organization has a computer that can give you the demographics of every village in Israel that needs the Gospel." But I say: why do we need a computer to tell us where to go, when all we have to do is open our ears and listen for God's direction and open our spiritual eyes to see what God is saying to us?

Dreams and visions fall into the category of the miraculous when supernatural revelations are imparted. The prophet Ezekiel enjoyed a continuous miracle ministry in the revelatory realm. God is raising up an "Ezekiel company" in our time empowered with the gifts of faith and the working of miracles. Believers' voices are often the trumpets that command the miraculous power of God. As we have traveled throughout the Holy Land and the Arab world with the Gospel, more than once we have been divinely led by drivers who testified with wonder and fear that they seemed to have been transported in a dream-like state to assist us.

MIRACLES OF TRANSPORT

Transportation miracles are reminiscent of Philip the evangelist in the New Testament. Philip was translated to Gaza by the Holy Spirit to meet an Ethiopian eunuch who was God-fearing, and who would subsequently spread the Gospel to Ethiopia. The Holy Spirit commanded Philip to join the Ethiopian's chariot so that he could teach him the Gospel.

The miracles of transportation in our ministry have involved Muslim drivers who seem to have been dreaming—literally!

One morning I decided to take a taxi to the American Colony Hotel for breakfast. A driver unknown to me was waiting in a van that morning outside of our ministry center, which at the time was located in Gethsemane's St. Stephen's Church. He was parked by the church, so I asked if his van was available.

"I don't know why I am here," he told me, very perplexed and disoriented, as if he had just awakened from a dream. "I don't work the day shift. All I can remember was that I was at home and in bed!"

"Well, where are you going now?" I asked.

"Home—to the Gihon Spring," he answered, and instantly the Holy Spirit prompted me to alter my plans and to "join this chariot," as Philip was commanded in Acts 8:29.

The Lord intended to use this driver to take me to an important venue. The outcome of my detour to the Gihon Spring was the first open-air Gospel meeting at this Biblical site near the ancient City of David perhaps since Bible times. Through a divine appointment with the taxi driver's friends, we discovered that the Jerusalem Municipality was constructing a new plaza at the Gihon Spring for Millennium pilgrims. Favor and permission were instantly granted that morning to organize an outdoor Gospel meeting in that plaza.

Having laid that groundwork, two years later we pitched a "Tabernacle of David" celebration also at the Gihon Spring, the original location of David's Tabernacle, with permission from the Orthodox Jewish community. It was a momentous prophetic occasion. One Orthodox Jew who attended commented, "Now that the Christians have restored the fallen tabernacle of David, it is a sure sign that the Jews should rebuild our Temple!"

While preparing for the Tabernacle of David, my husband and I heard some sounds of a saw in David's City. As we were producing a TV program, I went to investigate the sound, to ask if they could mute the sound for a few minutes. I discovered a man making Biblical Davidic harps. He said these harps were being prepared for the Third Temple endtime and that they were to be ready by a certain date—the same date we had set for our Tabernacle of David event! Needless to say, I invited the harp maker to play his very prophetic harp, and it happened right there in the Tabernacle at the Gihon Spring. And a taxi driver who had awakened from a trance as I walked out of the ministry center precipitated all of this!

ANOTHER DRIVER AWAKENS FROM A TRANCE

The following testimony happened a few years before the security wall was built at the entrance to Bethlehem. In those days there was a simple checkpoint of Israeli soldiers. A colleague and I needed a taxi to take us to scout Biblical Anathoth (Anata in Arabic) for a possible Gospel outreach. We had hailed many taxis, but no driver we had asked knew where Anata was located. As we were in Bethlehem at the time, a taxi driver dropped us at the checkpoint to find another driver who might know the way to Anata. Suddenly, a driver whom I had used occasionally seemed to awaken in broad daylight. He was parked near the checkpoint, where he recognized me and began calling my name.

"Christine! Christine!" My dazed taxi friend shouted from his window to get my attention. "I don't know how I got here! I don't remember driving here!" he said in a very bewildered manner, adding, "I feel like I have just awakened from a dream."

"But do you know the way to Anathoth?" I asked excitedly.

The puzzled driver—a man named Noor—muttered, "Yes!"

So I said, "Good! Don't worry. God sent you to us!"

And that is how the Spirit of God led us to scout Jeremiah's village of Anathoth—the driver seemed to have awakened from a trance. In Anathoth/Anata we later experienced one of our greatest Gospel outreaches among the Bedouin and Arab villagers there. We distributed so many Bibles that we almost created a traffic jam. People were following us and reaching for Bibles from out of our car windows. For that assignment, we felt it was only right to hire Noor for our driver, and God even used Noor at one point to translate while our regular translator was involved in an important phone call. Noor is a member of one of the Muslim families that God seems particularly to have his hand upon. As I have said, God is visiting Muslim families with the Gospel.

STRANGE SIGN AND WONDER IN NAZARETH

In another dramatic instance, a Muslim driver named Naim attempted to take our team after a day's holiday in Nazareth back to Jerusalem, but much to his consternation, our van repeatedly returned to the "welcome to Nazareth" sign at the city limits. This occurred five times over several hours. The disoriented driver was greatly shaken, because he was very familiar with the route to Jerusalem. Yet he could not fathom why his van was being transported back to the welcome sign against his wishes and careful driving.

Naim was extremely embarrassed and stopped the van by the side of the road to collect himself, shaking nervously. He covered his face with his hands, saying, "I seem to have lost control of this van. I don't know what to do."

We were also perplexed until it dawned on me that the Lord had previously spoken to a pastor to invite me to hold a Gospel outreach in Nazareth. So actually, it was the Lord's call. And I had not yet responded to Jesus of Nazareth to preach in his hometown! That particular day, my team had also noticed that I was hard of hearing. My ears seemed to be stopped up, but I was not physically sick.

Now I realized that we would not escape "the loop" until I said "Yes" to Jesus to preach in Nazareth! My stopped-up ears were a sign that apparently I had not heard, or properly responded, to His call to the Galilee. Indeed the Lord often communicates in "dark speech." (See an explanation of "dark speech" at the end of Chapter 4.)

But when I threw up my arms in resignation and said "Yes" to the assignment, suddenly my ears popped open, and the driver was released from invisible reins. Immediately, he was able once again to find his bearings! When we arrived at midnight in Jerusalem, Naim fell against the steering wheel and asked Jesus into his heart. He knew he had been moving in a supernatural realm. He began to drive our team regularly and often experienced comforting and edifying dreams from the Lord. Our eventual Gospel campaign, "Jesus of Nazareth Finds a Generation of Faith in Nazareth," resulted in people being saved and healed. We advertised in the press and on the radio, and our translator, an Anglican Arab pastor from the Galilee, was healed of a painful limp as he translated. It was wintertime, and he turned to see if his leg was hitting a radiator, but he said it was the heat of the Lord's hand as he was restored.

In their admirable prayer in Acts 4:30, the Apostles petitioned God for "signs and wonders." In the Old Testament the words for signs and wonders are 'oth ("sign," Strong's 226), meaning a signal, like a flag, a beacon, a mark, or a portent, and mofaith ("wonder," Strong's 4159), an event in the sense of being conspicuous.

In the New Testament, "sign" is semeion (Strong's 4592), used of miracles as signs of divine authority, and "wonder," teras (Strong's 5059), meaning "something strange," causing the beholder to marvel. According to Vine's Dictionary, a "sign" appeals to the understanding; a "wonder" appeals to the imagination; a "power" (dunamis) indicates the source is supernatural.

"Wonders" are mentioned as divine operations in 13 places in the New Testament, 9 of which are found in the Book of Acts. But here's an important cautionary note—three times "wonders" are ascribed to the work of satan through human agents (the false christs and false prophets of Matthew 24:24 and Mark 13:22; and the antichrist of 2 Thessalonians 2:9).

I believe we should claim "life verses" in the Bible with which we especially identify. One of my life verses is found in Isaiah 8:18:

> *"Behold, I and the children whom the Lord hath given me are for signs and for wonders in Israel from the Lord of hosts."*

The Hebrew word for "wonder" is sometimes rendered "portent." Portents in the heavens are end-time signs, according to Joel 2:30 and Acts 2:19, and we can experience these by faith. Here are some examples from our own ministry.

In Jerusalem, in 1995, at the time of our ninth spiritual warfare prayer meeting, which corresponded to the ninth plague of *dense darkness* in a very specific prayer strategy against the powers of darkness gripping the Middle East, there was a great portent over the region while we were engaged in corporate prayer. For the eight previous months we had been holding a series of progressive spiritual warfare prayer meetings, at the direction of the Holy Spirit, which He had named after the ten plagues of Egypt. The Lord indicated that each progressive prayer meeting would build in intensity and thus produce an accumulative effect in the heavens. When we reached the ninth prayer meeting, corresponding to the plague of "dense darkness," a lunar eclipse throughout the so-called 10/40 window on the world map coincided with our prayer service as a literal portent of actual darkness! The news media were full of the story.

It is, after all, not beyond the ability of the Creator to grant his children signs in the earth and in the sky. For a number of years the Lord called me to Africa, but on the day that the Lord allowed me to minister again in the Holy Land, a double rainbow appeared in the sky at the time of the meeting. When He called me to set up a ministry house again in Jerusalem, while I was pondering this direction with my husband in a car in England, a double rainbow appeared in the sky. Recently while preaching "down under" in Australia, a double rainbow appeared during our ministry tour, and so on—the incidents of double rainbows as "God's exclamation mark" to me are too numerous to recount here.

A portent can also be an indication or omen of something about to happen, especially something awesome or wonderful, and the dictionary also calls a portent a marvel, a sign, or a token.

In addition to dreams, visions, signs, wonders, and ministry gifts, however, love still remains the greatest gift.

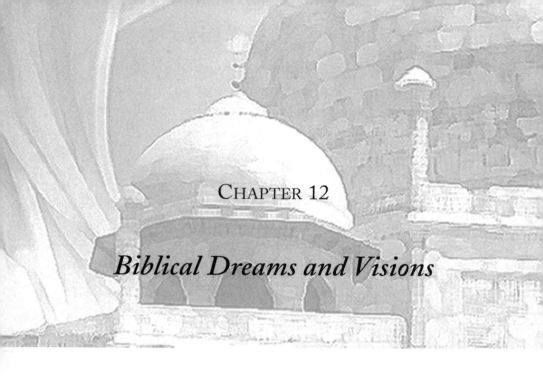

CHAPTER 12

Biblical Dreams and Visions

By examining the dreams recorded for our edification and admonition in Scripture, we understand that God speaks through dreams to all manner of men, women and children—whether they be kings, prophets, swindlers, cattle ranchers, bakers, butlers, soldiers, a man betrothed to be married, or the wife of a government official.

Here are the dreamers found in the Bible:

- *Abram.* In Genesis 15, God visited Abram in a vision that segued into a dream during which YHWH established the highly significant Abrahamic Covenant. This teaches us that God can make important transactions with his children through our dreams. God, therefore, sometimes accomplishes very significant life-altering and even potentially historic events within the realm of our dreams.

- *Abimelech*, a ruler, was prevented from sinning against Abram's wife because of a warning in a dream (Genesis 20:3).

- The patriarch *Jacob* dreamed of a supernatural ladder attended by angels and stretching into Heaven. He saw the Lord, who communicated comfort and direction and made a covenant with Jacob (Genesis 28:12).

  Jacob received in a dream the strategy to increase his livestock wealth (Genesis 46:2).

  Jacob received direction from God not to fear to travel to Egypt, for there in Egypt God would make of him a great nation (Genesis 46:2).

- *Laban*, a strong-willed man, received a directional warning from God not to hinder or speak negatively to his son-in-law, the Biblical patriarch Jacob (Genesis 31:24).

- *Joseph*, the favorite son of Jacob, dreamed prophetically of his future greatness and leadership when he envisioned his brethren as sheaves making obedience to his sheaf (Genesis 37:5).

  Joseph dreamed prophetically a second time of his family, represented by the sun, moon, and stars, bowing down to him (Genesis 37:9). Joseph's subsequent experience of rejection and hardship teaches us that it is not always wise to share our dreams prematurely with others.

- Egypt's chief *butler* dreamed prophetically a positive dream concerning his restoration and destiny as interpreted by Joseph in prison (Genesis 40:9).

- The chief *baker* of Egypt was also given a prophetic warning dream that did not have a happy ending (Genesis 40:16).

- Egypt's *Pharaoh* was granted a dream that warned of an impending famine (Genesis 41:1-4).

  There was a second dream of Pharaoh to emphasize that famine was surely coming (Genesis 41:5-8).

- *Gideon* providentially overheard the dream of a Midianite soldier that assured Gideon of victory in battle (Judges 7:13).

- God appeared to King *Solomon* in a dream to test his desires; Solomon communicated back to God asking for wisdom, and his desire was rewarded plus more. This passage of Scripture teaches us that it is possible for God to grant gifts in our dreams and that our spirits can respond in a godly manner even when we are experiencing deep sleep (1 Kings 3:3-15).

- *Eliphaz*, one of Job's "comforters," described a visitation from a spirit in a night vision and a voice that he heard from God (Job 4:12-21).

- *Job* experienced nightmares and stated that dreams symbolize the short-lived pleasures of the wicked (Job 7:14; 20:8).

- King *Nebuchadnezzar* dreamed prophetically of world kingdoms (Daniel 2) and concerning himself (Daniel 4).

- *Daniel* dreamed prophetically of destinies of kingdoms and received much apocalyptic information concerning Messiah and the Last Days. Furthermore, Daniel possessed the power and gift to interpret dreams (Daniel 1:17; 2:1-3; 7, 8, 10:5-9).

- The prophet *Joel* affirmed that dreams and visions would be one of the Last Days provisions of the Holy Spirit (Joel 2:28).

- In the New Testament, St. *Joseph* was instructed in a divine dream not to fear to marry the Virgin Mary because her child was conceived by the Holy Spirit (Matthew 1:20).

  Joseph, as head of the household, was warned in a dream to escape with Mary and the Baby Jesus to Egypt (Matthew 2:13).

Furthermore, Joseph was granted the "all clear" in a dream to return home with the holy family (Matthew 2:19). Joseph received news of wicked King Herod's death in this timely dream.

- The *Wise Men* who traveled to worship Jesus were warned in a dream to return in another direction to evade the wicked designs of murderous King Herod (Matthew 2:12).

- *Pilate's wife* warned her husband, the Roman governor, not to harm Jesus on the day of His crucifixion because of what she had suffered in a dream (Matthew 27:19).

- The Apostle *Paul* received specific guidance through a dream by a man beckoning him to bring the Gospel to Macedonia (Acts 16:9). Thus Christianity, which began as an Eastern movement, spread westward to Europe because of a dream.

  Paul was assured in a dream that it was God's plan and purpose for his life that he should take the Gospel to Rome (Acts 23:11).

  Furthermore, Paul was given assurance of safety for himself and for all sailors during a shipwreck (Acts 28:23-24).

Both Joseph, who became prime minister of Egypt, and Daniel, who ruled in Babylon, possessed a supernatural gift that enabled them to interpret the disturbing dreams of Pharaoh and Nebuchadnezzar. It is important to note that they credited the Spirit of God with their ability to interpret the dreams that nobody else could interpret. We must also ask God to grant us by his Spirit this ability when needed. Jesus said that we have not simply because we ask not.

It must be reiterated that we do not need today to depend upon dreams, visions, and voices, because as the Apostle Peter declared in the New Testament, we have a "more sure word of prophecy" and "exceedingly great and precious promises" in the Bible to guide us. *But not everybody in this world has access to the Bible.* The manner in which an important message was conveyed to Eliphaz in Job chapter 4 has many salient points of a visitation by God or a ministering spirit in a night vision:

> *Now a thing was secretly brought to me, and my ear received a whisper of it.*
>
> *In thoughts from the visions of the night, when deep sleep falls on men,*
>
> *Fear came upon me and trembling, which made all my bones shake.*
>
> *Then a spirit passed before my face; the hair of my flesh stood up!*
>
> *[The spirit] stood still, but I could not discern the appearance of it. A form was before my eyes; there was silence, and then I heard a voice, saying,*
>
> *Can mortal man be just before God, or be more right than He is? Can a man be pure before his Maker, or be more cleansed than He is?*
>
> *Even in His [heavenly] servants He puts no trust or confidence, and His angels He charges with folly and error—*
>
> *How much more those who dwell in houses (bodies) of clay, whose foundations are in the dust, who are crushed like the moth.*
>
> *Between morning and evening they are destroyed; without anyone noticing it they perish forever. Is not their tent cord plucked up within them [so that the tent falls]? Do they not die, and that without [acquiring] wisdom?* (Job 4:12-21 Amplified Bible)

SECRET FRIENDSHIP OF THE LORD

First of all, let us observe that the message above was *communicated secretly*. Someone has said, "In sleep and in the night, my heavenly Lord may drop His hints into my soul, showing me how I should live and act in broad day." However, in many countries, there is great persecution if a believer puts his faith in Jesus. God has given many revelations in secret, where no eye sees, and the Holy Spirit of God has hidden ways of bringing counsel and comfort to his chosen ones, unobserved by the world.

These private revelations are just as significant as public ministry. In fact, Psalm 25:24 declares that the "secret of the Lord is with them that fear him." One commentator has aptly said, "As the evil spirit often steals good words out of the heart (Matthew 13:19), so the good Spirit sometimes steals good words into the heart"—words of which no friend, family, or foe are aware. Daniel 2:19 says, "Then was the secret revealed unto Daniel in a night vision. Then Daniel blessed the God of Heaven." God revealed great future events to the prophet Daniel, which were secrets that were sealed until the endtime, when they will be revealed to the world.

Moreover, notice in Job chapter 4 concerning revelations to Eliphaz, that God spoke during "deep slumber," (i.e. REM sleep), when man is not jabbering and he is quieted to hear from the Almighty.

Observe also that the night vision resulted in fear and trembling, not craven fear, but rather *a holy, reverential fear,* a sure sign that a dream or vision is directed from God.

Thirdly, note what I call an *"audible silence"* before the ministering spirit communicated. An almost tangible silence before God speaks is often a characteristic of a supernatural encounter with the Lord.

Visions or Trance-like State

Now let's turn to visions, which usually occur while a person is awake or in what the New Testament calls a "trance." According to the Dake Annotated Reference Bible, several Hebrew words are translated as "vision":

- *Chazon*, a mental sight, dream, revelation, oracle. This could come in the form of a divine utterance of words, such as a dream, a writing, or a mental picture while one is awake.

- *Chezev*, a night vision. This word is used of visions while asleep, known as dreams or night visions.

- *Marah*, a vision as seeing something in a mirror, appearance.

- *Mareh*, sight; appearance.

Men and women from all walks of life in the Old Testament experienced visions (supernatural vignettes and mental images). And in the New Testament, the Lord Jesus and the disciples experienced visions. All were recorded for our admonition and instruction:

- The patriarch *Abraham* was promised an heir and descendants as numerous as the stars and a land in an expansive vision of destiny (Genesis 15).

- The visionary prophet *Balaam* was warned not to curse Israel as the Lord spoke to him in the realm of "seeing" (Numbers 24:4).

- The call of the boy prophet *Samuel* is described as a vision (1 Samuel 3:1,15).

- Received by vision, *Nathan* the prophet announced God's perpetual plans to bless King David's house (2 Samuel 7:17; 1 Chronicles 17:15).

- *Isaiah*, son of Amoz, beheld visions concerning Judah and Jerusalem during the reigns of Uzziah, Jotham, Ahaz, and Hezekiah, kings of Judah, and concerning the holiness of the Lord (Isaiah 1:1; 6:1; 2 Chronicles 32:32).

- The Prophet *Ezekiel* was granted extraordinary "Technicolor" visions of God, his throne, the living creatures, and of Jerusalem and the Temple (Ezekiel 1:1; 40).

- *Iddo*, an Old Testament "seer," experienced visions concerning Jeroboam, son of Nebat (2 Chronicles 9:29).

- The Prophet *Daniel* was granted extraordinary visions to interpret the king's dreams and visions concerning future empires, the Messiah, angels, spiritual warfare, and the endtime (Daniel 2:19; 8:1-27; 9:21-24).

- King *Nebuchadnezzar* experienced both dreams and visions concerning a mysterious image emblematic of world empires (Daniel 2:28).

- The vision of the Prophet *Obadiah* concerned Edom (Obadiah 1).

- The vision of the Prophet *Nahum* concerned Nineveh (Nahum 1:1).

- *Habakkuk,* a visionary prophet, received instructions to write his vision and to make it plain upon tablets (Habakkuk 2:2-3).

- *Jesus Christ* received words of knowledge concerning His disciples and others by visions. All of His ministry instructions from the Father were perceived by vision. "Verily, verily, I say unto you, The Son can do nothing of himself, but what he seeth the Father do: for what things soever He doeth, these also doeth the Son likewise" (John 5:19; 8:38). Jesus told Nathanael that He had seen him by vision under a fig tree before they had met (John 1:48).

- *Peter* the apostle beheld Jesus, Moses, and Elijah on the Mount of Transfiguration and was commissioned in a visionary trance to preach to the Gentiles (Matthew 17:9; Acts 10:19; 11:5).

- *James* the apostle beheld the transfigured Messiah conversing with Moses and Elijah (Matthew 17:9).

- *John* the apostle witnessed the Transfiguration and the extraordinary visions of the Book of Revelation (Matthew 17:9; Revelation 1:1-2; 9:17).

- *Zacharias,* the priest and father of John the Baptist, saw a vision of the angel Gabriel, who announced the birth of John the Baptist (Luke 1:22).

- *Ananias,* a disciple of Jesus in Damascus, was commissioned in a vision to minister to the Church's persecutor, Saul of Tarsus (Acts 9:10-12).

- *Cornelius,* a Roman Centurion, was chosen in a vision because of his prayers and alms to organize the first house meeting for the Gospel to be preached to the Gentiles (Acts 10:3,17).

- The apostle *Paul* encountered the Risen Jesus on the Damascus Road and was granted many revelations by visions (Acts 16:9-10; 18:9; 2 Corinthians 12:1-9).

Let's examine the first vision recorded in the Bible in Genesis 15:1-16, for contained therein are salient points concerning visions:

After these things the word of the Lord came unto Abram in a vision, saying, Fear not, Abram: I am thy shield, and thy exceeding great reward. And Abram said, Lord God, what wilt Thou give me, seeing I go childless, and the steward of my house is this Eliezer of Damascus? And Abram said, Behold, to me Thou hast given no seed: and, lo, one born in my house is mine heir. And, behold, the word of the Lord came unto him, saying, This shall not be thine heir; but he that shall come forth out of thine own bowels shall be thine heir. And he brought him forth abroad, and said, Look now toward Heaven, and tell the stars, if thou be able to number them: and he said unto him, So shall thy seed be. And he believed in the Lord; and He counted it to him for righteousness. And he said unto him, I am the Lord that brought thee out of Ur of the Chaldees, to give thee this land to inherit it. And he said, Lord God, whereby shall I know that I shall inherit it? And He said unto him, Take me an heifer of three years old, and a she goat of three years old, and a ram of three years old, and a turtledove, and a young pigeon. And he took unto him all these, and divided them in the midst, and laid each piece one against another: but the birds divided he not. And when the fowls came down upon the carcases, Abram drove them away. And when the sun was going down, a deep sleep fell upon Abram; and, lo, an horror of great darkness fell upon him. And He said unto Abram, Know of a surety that thy seed shall be a stranger in a land that is not theirs, and shall serve them; and they shall afflict them four hundred years; And also that nation, whom they shall serve, will I judge: and afterward shall they come out with great substance. And thou shalt go to thy fathers in peace; thou shalt be buried in a good old age. But in the fourth generation they shall come hither again: for the iniquity of the Amorites is not yet full.

VISIONARY REALM IS OFTEN A TWO-WAY EXCHANGE

Notice, first of all, that God assures Abram not to be afraid; inordinate fear is a factor that must be reckoned with in the visionary realm. Then the Lord commences to commune with Abram. But Abram also communes with God—it is a "two-way street" of revelation between God and His servant in the vision. Part of visionary experiences, therefore, is the exchange of communications between God and believers.

The Lord offers words of encouragement and also shows Abram his destiny and calling and reveals many details to come. Righteousness is imputed to Abram in the vision because he exercised faith in the visionary realm and "believed God." This teaches us that we can make definite faith exchanges during times of visionary revelation, as well as times when we are fully awake.

Note also that the vision took place over many hours. When the sun was setting, the vision mode changed into a deep sleep mode—the experience moved from the visionary realm in verse 1 into a REM dream mode in verse 12. Therefore, the combined experiences of Abram's visions and dreams in Genesis chapter 15 probably lasted 24 hours! God revealed his purposes not only for Abram's entire life but also for his descendants, so it was no wonder that the vision lasted for many hours continuously. From this we learn that visions are not always a short flash of illumination. I can attest that once I experienced a vision on a transatlantic flight that lasted nearly seven hours (concerning plans for a conference in Jerusalem).

In the New Testament, we are informed in John 16:13 that the Spirit of God will reveal "things to come." God will first speak through the voice of the Spirit, but because we are often dull of hearing, he may resort to speaking to us in startling dream pictures.

Graciously, the Holy Spirit may show us a solution to a difficult situation in a dream, revealing important steps to take. At times we see ourselves speaking in a dream, a revelation of what we must do or not do. The Holy Spirit inspires us to give an answer fitting in with God's plan. Sometimes, God may grant us an awesome vision of his glory, as was the humbling experience of the prophet Isaiah (chapter 6:1), or we may be astonished and anguished by what we see for days on end, as were the experiences of Ezekiel and Daniel. They were incapacitated because of the magnitude of the visions they beheld.

It is exciting to contemplate that although men and women from all walks of life received dreams and visions in the Bible, we are promised in the Last Days that both men and women, as well as old men and young men, will especially experience dreams and visions. The next chapter will examine some of the potential pitfalls.

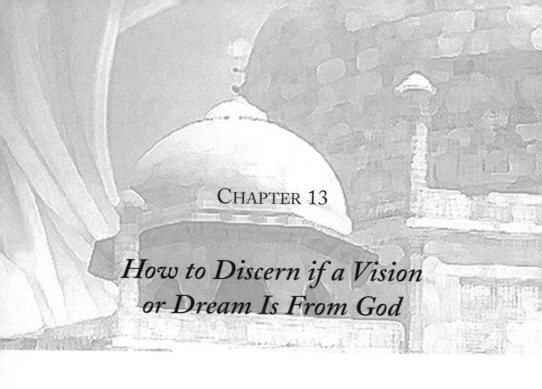

CHAPTER 13

How to Discern if a Vision or Dream Is From God

Beloved, believe not every spirit, but try the spirits whether they are of God: because many false prophets are gone out into the world. Hereby know ye the Spirit of God: Every spirit that confesseth that Jesus Christ is come in the flesh is of God: And every spirit that confesseth not that Jesus Christ is come in the flesh is not of God: and this is that spirit of antichrist, whereof ye have heard that it should come; and even now already is it in the world (1 John 4:1-3).

When you hear that God is granting souls an abundance of dreams and visions, particularly in the Muslim world, you must never beg the Lord to lead you by this path. Such a desire may reveal a lack of humility and can even expose you to the peril of deception.

The highest form of faith believes without seeing. Jesus said, "Blessed are they that have not seen, and yet have believed." (John 20:29). The Bible is all the proof you need that Jesus is alive and that He is Lord. The New Testament is the Holy Spirit-breathed record of eyewitnesses of Jesus'

sinless life, death, and Resurrection. He is "the same yesterday, and to
day, and for ever" (Hebrews 13:8).

It can be dangerous to focus one's spiritual life on dreams and visions, hoping for special revelations.

*All dreams and visions are subject to the test of the Word. Any revelation
through a dream or a vision, or a word of prophecy—no matter how spectacular or supernatural—outside of the Word of God must be judged. We are
commanded in the Bible to test the spirits.*

Dreams and visions are certainly to be expected in the Spirit-filled
life of all believers, according to Acts 2:17. They are the methods that
God has used frequently to speak to people throughout the ages. Secular humanism has conditioned us to treat as suspect knowledge that
does not originate from the five senses. Yet picture language in the
Bible is the language of the Spirit.

Perhaps you have experienced a dream or a vision and wonder if it
was truly "from God" or perhaps from a *jinn* (a spirit of questionable
origin), or perhaps it was merely a result of your thought patterns during the day.

Perhaps you have experienced a recurring dream. If you determine
that the source of the dream or vision was from the Spirit of God, you
will be very wise to take heed to the message and to obey it. If the
dream or vision, on the other hand, is the result of a "familiar spirit"
(i.e., a demonic spirit that is "familiar" with your life and circumstances) then you must resist the dream or vision and cancel its troubling effects through prayer. The Bible gives a strong warning against
dabbling in the occult, which can result in a person being visited and
tormented by familiar spirits:

*And when they shall say unto you, Seek unto them that have famil-
iar spirits, and unto wizards that peep, and that mutter: should not
a people seek unto their God? for the living to the dead? To the law
and to the testimony: if they speak not according to this word, it is
because there is no light in them* (Isaiah 8:19-20).

Certain patterns emerged in the various incidents reported in this volume. Many persons over the course of time have experienced the same dreams and visions about Jesus more than once. There is a principle set down in the Bible, mentioned in the book of Genesis by the dreamer Joseph, who was endowed with the gift of dream interpretation, *that if a dream comes from God it could be repeated more than once.* When the Egyptian Pharaoh dreamed about forthcoming famine, the message from God was repeated in two different dream parables because the future event was "established by God" and would shortly come to pass (Genesis 41:32).

So recurring dreams, especially about the Lord, can be highly significant—don't ignore them! Seek God and pray it through. *A dream that originates from God will leave you with a deep feeling of peace and purpose; it will leave an indelible impression upon your spirit that will not go away but will grow.*

Ever since I was a teenager, I have experienced awesome dreams of the Second Coming of Jesus. I have seen Him descending in the clouds with great glory and authority. These dreams have strengthened my faith in Jesus as the risen Lord and coming King. I have never doubted that these dreams originated from a heavenly source, because the Bible confirms the truth of the Second Coming. In fact, the doctrine of the Second Coming of Jesus is one of the greatest historic and orthodox doctrines of the Church.

Nightmares, on the other hand, can be demonic and must be resisted and stopped by prayer. You must *actively refuse* to accept disturbing interruptions of peaceful sleep by demonic invasion! I related earlier in this book about a young man who was tormented by a recurring nightmare. When we prayed in the name of Jesus and took authority over the demonic attack, the nightmares stopped immediately.

The Blood of Jesus is a powerful spiritual weapon that never fails to protect. Before going to sleep at night, commit your body, soul, and spirit to the Lord and ask that only He communicate with you. Draw the "bloodline" of the protection of Jesus, and do not allow demonic influences to disturb your sleep. Learn to use the authority of the name of Jesus to command all disturbances to leave you at once.

When my husband and I were staying with our young boys many years ago in a Cypriot hotel room, one night a demonic presence came into the room. My husband sat up in bed and demanded the presence to leave immediately in the name of Jesus, and the door banged shut! Since then we have learned to cleanse our hotel rooms spiritually through prayer and the name of Jesus.

In childhood we often experience a fine line between reality and the realm of our imaginations. We must also take into account the possibility of an overactive imagination in some persons, even adults. The human personality can be very susceptible to imaginations. Even hallucinations can be the result of abstinence and weakness through fasting. Some persons have used their imaginations to invent stories. About 10 years ago, a former nun visited Jerusalem and claimed to have met with a rabbi who gave her many "revelations," which tickled the ears of many believers. Even though at the time the incident was reported as fact, I felt in my spirit that her stories were not true. Now she is claiming that the events were not actually real but visionary.

Demonic sources may give false visions or revelations, as was the case of the well-documented nun "Magdalen of the Cross." She was a Spanish Franciscan nun who lived at the beginning of the sixteenth century, who faked stigmata of the wounds of Jesus and who managed to persuade others that she lived without food while procuring it for herself secretly. She had entered into a pact with the devil in order to gain fame as a saint.

Therefore, we need to watch out for the work of satan—he may really promote good things for a while, provided that in the long run he gains.

Smith Wigglesworth and the Devil

English Evangelist Smith Wigglesworth was fearless as he prayed for the sick and performed apostolic exploits for the Lord. Wigglesworth's grandson, Leslie, personally related an incident when I produced a TV documentary on Smith Wigglesworth. One night

Smith Wigglesworth was sleeping in a drafty room during a thunderstorm. The windows rattled, the lights flickered, and suddenly Wigglesworth saw a vision of satan standing at the foot of his bed! But Wigglesworth was not in the least bit disturbed. Because he possessed such a revelation of personal safety under the watchcare of the Good Shepherd, and because he understood the power of the name of Jesus, Wigglesworth just dismissed the devil. He said, "Oh, it's only you!" He turned over in his bed and fell into a deep slumber!

We must underline the Biblical principle that God seals our instructions often when we are fully surrendered in deep sleep. A dream is ordinarily not God's primary way of speaking to us—He may first speak to us through His Word and through His still, small voice. But often, because we are dull of hearing, or simply because we are not listening, or because somebody does not have access to the Word of God, the Lord in His love and mercy employs the means of speaking to our spirits. After all, our spirits are alive and never sleep, and they can be contacted through dreams, night visions, or "similitudes" (mental pictures, images).

We learn this very salient point from Job 33:15-16: "In a dream, in a vision of the night, when deep sleep falleth upon men, in slumberings upon the bed; Then he openeth the ears of men, and sealeth their instruction." Thus through dreams and night visions, the Lord God admonishes men by their consciences, in secret whispers, which any man or woman of wisdom will hear and heed.

On the other hand, most of our dreams are merely colored by the events of our daily lives. According to Ecclesiastes 5:7, it is important to note that some dreams are simply the result of *various vanities*: "For in the multitude of dreams and many words there are also divers vanities: but fear thou God."

Job 33:14-23 is an important passage of Scripture for understanding how and why God speaks to us in dreams:

> *For God speaketh once, yea twice, yet man perceiveth it not. In a dream, in a vision of the night, when deep sleep falleth upon men, in slumberings upon the bed; Then he openeth the ears of men, and sealeth their instruction, That he may withdraw man*

from his purpose, and hide pride from man. He keepeth back his soul from the pit, and his life from perishing by the sword. He is chastened also with pain upon his bed, and the multitude of his bones with strong pain: So that his life abhorreth bread, and his soul dainty meat. His flesh is consumed away, that it cannot be seen; and his bones that were not seen stick out. Yea, his soul draweth near unto the grave, and his life to the destroyers. If there be a messenger with him, an interpreter, one among a thousand, to shew unto man his uprightness.

In the above passage we see that God graciously and mercifully speaks again and again to us, in dreams, in visions of the night when deep sleep falls, during what the scientists call REM (rapid eye movement) sleep. God opens our ears in times like that and imparts to us wisdom and instruction, causing us to "wake up" and to change our minds, restraining us therefore from the dangerous sin of pride, and warning us of the penalties of sin, or preventing us from falling into a tragic trap.

God's methods have not changed, for he says, "I am the Lord, I change not" (Malachi 3:6). In the above Job passage, we learn that all people dream and are thus susceptible to receiving letter pictures from God. Some people tell me that they never dream. They are simply not remembering their dreams, because scientists inform us that all people dream every night. However, dreams that originate from us or from a distraught day or from indigestion will not be long remembered. A supernatural dream, on the other hand, will be remembered. Some we will remember all of our lives because of the impact of God-sent dreams.

Furthermore, we learn from this passage of Scripture in the Book of Job that God allows sickness and pain to the point that we may lose our appetites and even perhaps become so ill that we are reduced to mere skin and bones as we draw near to the gates of death. This in turn causes us to seek the Lord and to develop a prayer life. And if an interpreter of dreams—a rare commodity—can be found to show us what is right, then our chastened bodies will become as healthy as a child's, firm and youthful again. Yes, God often does these things for man— brings back his soul from the Pit, so that he may live.

So a dream comes once, twice, to deliver us from our own destructive ways.

Whenever God outpours his Spirit, dreams and visions become a part of the move of God, but these phenomena are especially a Last Days characteristic, according to the prophecies in Joel 2:28 and Acts 2:17: "And it shall come to pass afterward, that I will pour out my spirit upon all flesh; and your sons and your daughters shall prophesy, your old men shall dream dreams, your young men shall see visions."

True Biblical dreams and visions are therefore often the result of the gracious outpouring of the Holy Spirit and are part of every move of God. The enemy will always counterfeit the genuine moves of God, but that does not change God's willingness to use and speak through visions and dreams. It is our duty not to resist the gracious Spirit of God when he deals with us privately through these means.

PRAY FOR THE GIFT OF DISCERNING OF SPIRITS

Today there is an insatiable interest in the supernatural, in angels, apparitions, demons, psychic hotlines, the occult and the paranormal, prophecies, astrology, mediums, UFOs, "holy" men, fakirs, spiritual "channels," and so on.

There is therefore much increasing delusion in the world. People believe there are many paths to God outside of the Way and the Door, Jesus the Messiah. They believe that if their good actions outweigh their bad, they will somehow earn the right to enter the portals of Heaven. Even some of the most vile and wicked persons delude themselves because of "pop theology," believing that they are protected by guardian angels, or that they will somehow slip into Heaven through a back door when they die.

But the New Testament teaches that angels are "ministering spirits" unto the "heirs of salvation" (Hebrews 1:14), those who trust completely in the Atonement of Jesus the Messiah. "There is a way that seemeth right unto a man, but the end thereof are the ways of death" (Proverbs 16:25).

Much of the supernatural concerning angels depicted in the media is not of a Biblical origin, but the proliferation of the paranormal does underscore the great hunger that exists in the world for the supernatural. This is why we must also hunger and thirst for *the gift of the discerning of spirits* to be able to detect accurately what phenomena are godly, what is simply an outcome of the natural world, and what originates from the demonic realm. The gift of the discerning of spirits (i.e., what kind of spirit is communicating with you or dominates a person) is listed in the New Testament as an enablement of the Holy Spirit. All believers should earnestly covet these spiritual gifts from God:

> *But the manifestation of the Spirit is given to every man to profit withal. For to one is given by the Spirit the word of wisdom; to another the word of knowledge by the same Spirit; To another faith by the same Spirit; to another the gifts of healing by the same Spirit; To another the working of miracles; to another prophecy; to another discerning of spirits; to another divers kinds of tongues; to another the interpretation of tongues* (1 Corinthians 12:7-10).

The Lord established communication principles in the Torah, stating some of the ways that He would make Himself known to mankind:

> *And He said, Hear now My words: If there be a prophet among you, I the Lord will make Myself known unto him in a vision, and will speak unto him in a dream. My servant Moses is not so, who is faithful in all Mine house. With him will I speak mouth to mouth, even apparently, and not in dark speeches; and the similitude of the Lord shall he behold* (Numbers 12:6-8).

Before sin entered the world, divine guidance through dreams and visions was not necessary. Adam and Eve enjoyed perfect and intimate communication with God so that there was no need for "dark speech," similitudes, dreams, and visions. However, when man was alienated from God through his fall into sin, the Lord in his mercy reached out and spoke to mankind by anointing and sending prophets, by commissioning His written Word, and by speaking through the gifts of the Spirit, including dreams and visions.

God says He will not always speak to us face to face. In the above passage, God explains that He will make his will known and seal the instructions of many who are destined to become His messengers, His "preachers." By noting that He favored Moses by speaking "mouth to mouth," that is, "face to face," He also revealed that with others who do not hear Him so clearly, He will speak with "dark sayings" and similitudes.

Why? These mental images, parables in picture, or puzzlements are meant to "bait" us, in a sense, to entice us to seek more intensely after the Lord in fervent prayer. These "dark sayings" are almost like qualifying tests to see how hungry we are to receive more from the Lord. Unspiritual, casual souls will not seek the Lord further in prayer and will not press through to gain additional clarifying insights from the Lord. Thus they eliminate themselves from much fruitfulness and opportunity in the Lord's service.

In the Old Testament the prophet Daniel experienced many visions, but he diligently sought the Lord through prayer and fasting for the interpretations. God may give you a vision, but he may also require you to seek for the meaning. If we will faithfully pray and fast if necessary, the faithful Lord will grant us light.

Many times the Lord will speak in a dream to avert disaster; we must not ignore these communications. Even our subconscious will speak to us in a dream if we are about to embark on a decision with which our spirit man or the Holy Spirit do not agree. A person who has made a wrong decision in an engagement to be married, for example, or in a career move, may receive a disturbing dream as a warning, which he or she must not ignore.

OBEYING THE HEAVENLY VISION

When we discern that a vision or dream originates from God, it is vitally important that we, like the Apostle Paul, obey our heavenly vision. Summoned to make an answer for himself before King Agrippa, Paul gave this testimony concerning his commission from Jesus to preach the Gospel:

And when we were all fallen to the earth, I heard a voice speaking unto me, and saying in the Hebrew tongue, Saul, Saul, why persecutest thou Me? it is hard for thee to kick against the pricks. And I said, Who art thou, Lord? And He said, I am Jesus whom thou persecutest. But rise, and stand upon thy feet: for I have appeared unto thee for this purpose, to make thee a minister and a witness both of these things which thou hast seen, and of those things in the which I will appear unto thee; Delivering thee from the people, and from the Gentiles, unto whom now I send thee, To open their eyes, and to turn them from darkness to light, and from the power of Satan unto God, that they may receive forgiveness of sins, and inheritance among them which are sanctified by faith that is in Me. Whereupon, O king Agrippa, I was not disobedient unto the heavenly vision (Acts 26:14-19).

Some people say they were shown in a vision to preach in Africa or elsewhere, but they are uncertain if it was God or satan speaking to them. But does satan ever call anybody to preach the Gospel and to minister to the lost? The devil hates the Gospel! Note that in the above vision, the Lord and Paul conversed with one another. It was a "two-way street" of communication on the Damascus Road. Also in the vision Jesus informed Paul that He would appear unto him again to give further instructions. Therefore we can count on the Lord's guidance as often as it is needed.

The following passage from Habakkuk 2:1-3 contains some of the most important and insightful verses in the Bible concerning the reception and outworking of heavenly visions:

- *I will stand upon my watch, and set me upon the tower, and will watch to see what he will say unto me, and what I shall answer when I am reproved.*

- *And the Lord answered me, and said, Write the vision, and make it plain upon tables, that he may run that readeth it.*

- *For the vision is yet for an appointed time, but at the end it shall speak, and not lie: though it tarry, wait for it; because it will surely come, it will not tarry.*

From the above verses, we learn that, as we watch and pray, we will "see" something as the Lord speaks to us during a time of exhortation and reproving. We learn that whatever vision or dream the Lord grants should be recorded plainly and that all visions from the Lord will come to pass at His appointed time without disappointments or delay. Let God fulfill every vision in its time!

GOD CHERISHES HIS OWN DREAMS ABOUT YOU

A precious Biblical truth is that God Himself envisions and cherishes dreams for our lives! The Psalmist proclaimed that while we were just beginning in our mothers' wombs,

> *Thine eyes did see my substance, yet being unperfect; and in Thy book all my members were written....How precious also are Thy thoughts unto me, O God!* (Psalm 139:16-17)

And in the following verse, the Lord revealed that he envisions special plans for every life:

> *For I know the thoughts that I think toward you, saith the Lord, thoughts of peace, and not of evil, to give you an expected end. Then shall ye call upon Me, and ye shall go and pray unto Me, and I will hearken unto you. And ye shall seek Me, and find Me, when ye shall search for Me with all your heart* (Jeremiah 29:11-13).

Therefore, we must petition the Lord to open our eyes to behold the special visions and dreams that He has preordained and planned for our individual lives. Like the prophet Habakkuk, let's start to look "to *see* what God will *say* to us!"

STEPS TO RECALL YOUR VISIONS AND DREAMS

1. Before retiring to bed or finishing a prayer time, ask the Lord to sanctify your time of sleep and to commune with your soul and spirit in the night watches.

2. As an act of your will, command yourself to remember your dream or anything else the Lord shows you. This is an act of faith that will send a signal to your spirit to stay alert.

3. Keep a journal of every prophetic word, impression, vision, or dream that you receive from the Lord. Even though you assume at the time that you will remember all the details of even spectacular visions and dreams, chances are you will not recall everything. That is why it is important to record the details immediately so nothing will be lost. When attempting to recall an important dream or vision, close your eyes and review every scene and impression before recording the details.

WHAT SHOULD BE YOUR RESPONSE?

After you have determined that the source of your dream or vision is divine, pray for the proper understanding and interpretation, as well as the timing of your response. Petition the Holy Spirit to help you with the interpretation. Seek the counsel of more mature, godly believers.

If you believe Jesus has been communicating with you, pray for courage to respond in faith to the dream or vision. If He is calling you to follow Him, please note the following strong words of our Lord in Luke 14:26-28 concerning the cost of discipleship:

> *If any man come to Me, and hate not his father, and mother, and wife, and children, and brethren, and sisters, yea, and his own life also, he cannot be My disciple. And whosoever doth not bear his cross, and come after Me, cannot be My disciple. For which of you, intending to build a tower, sitteth not down first, and counteth the cost, whether he have sufficient to finish it?*

In these words Jesus is not demanding that we must literally hate our families, but rather He used a Hebrew *idiomatic expression of preference*—meaning that we must prefer Him above all earthly persons and relationships.

CHAPTER 14

Revival Epilogue

May there be many more dreams and visions that lost souls might behold the Lamb of God who takes away the sins of the world!

But remember—the Gospel is not normally preached through dreams and visions. The unexaggerated testimonies in this book are only evidences of the mercy and grace of God as the endtime is almost fulfilled.

We still must bear our solemn responsibility and duty to make disciples of all nations and to preach the Gospel by all means possible. After you have heard the call of God to deliver the captives, the Lord may give you a personal vision as a confirmation of the territory to which He is sending you.

But do not seek visions; the only vision we need is to be fulfillers of the Great Commission. Without the Biblical vision to preach, the people will perish. And if the Lord gives you a vision to evangelize the lost and dying, to heal the sick and hurting, whatever you do, determine to be faithful like the Apostle Paul who declared in Acts 26:19, "I was not disobedient unto the heavenly vision."

THE REVIVAL CONTINUES

The move of the Holy Spirit that began in Arabia is continuing at a school administered by Asians and Arabs. The staff is experiencing revival that started among Muslim children (many of whom by now have returned to their home countries). The children have taken the testimonies of their personal encounter and knowledge of Jesus back to their Muslim lands.

In 1994, Jesus Himself appeared in a white Middle Eastern robe to an entire classroom of Muslim pupils and taught them about the Holy Bible. Subsequently that room was set aside for prayer as a chapel to seek the Lord's face.

The school invited me to hold further revival meetings. The Holy Spirit ministered with many manifestations, something similar to what had happened at the beginning of the revival.

When I returned a few years later, it was a privilege to preach under the portrait of the Middle Eastern leader, a benign-looking emir who, in his white headdress, resembled a Biblical patriarch. Once again the atmosphere in the school hall where we held the meetings was filled with the wafting fragrance of the Rose of Sharon!

Many of us smelled the rose of Sharon fragrance and felt His tangible presence. We were awed by the presence of the Holy Spirit. Many testified to being freed from longstanding infirmities.

But, as in any genuine revival, the greatest manifestations were the instances of salvation, particularly among the staff, and especially the men, who sat, arms rigidly folded across their chests, in the back of the hall. Some attended the revival meetings only because attendance was compulsory. These schoolmasters were rigid and unyielding—until the Holy Ghost fell upon them with convicting revival fire!

Some of the men were also new staff masters who had never experienced the previous revival, let alone spiritual rebirth! (The school's staff of expatriates is constantly changing.)

Graciously, the Holy Spirit broke down their hardness or uncertainties, and they began to shake with great conviction of sin. It was like a scene I had read about in the Welsh revival and other revivals— a sovereign move of God. It proved to me how easy it is to preach and to get results when revival falls and when revival has been properly prepared!

The first man who ran forward to repent confessed openly to an adulterous relationship, which he resolved to break immediately. He told me later that a great burden of sin and guilt had been removed, and he was restored to his wife.

Another of the schoolmasters on the back row began to convulse with remorse, and although he had secretly vowed he would never testify publicly because of his pride, he nevertheless ran forward to the front of the room where we were standing and preaching. He renounced pornography videos that had been polluting him and his family.

The repentant schoolmaster had just seen a terrible vision of himself sitting in front of his TV set. And he heard a voice declare, "It were better for him that a millstone were hanged about his neck, and he cast into the sea, than that he should offend one of these little ones" (Luke 17:2).

As in many Middle Eastern settings, the men were seated separately from the women. When the men melted from their hardness of heart and rushed forward from the back of the room, one by one, weeping, to publicly acknowledge Jesus, those in the women's section took fresh courage. None needed to be led in a sinner's prayer. The power of God was upon each one to such a degree that they individually began to confess sins and to call upon the name of the Lord, praying fervently from their hearts.

This, in turn, broke the floodgates, and also many Hindus, who had been holding back, particularly among the female staff, knelt down and confessed Jesus as Lord. The Holy Spirit had broken down even the most resistant ones under the power of my text, Matthew 10:32: "Whosoever therefore shall confess Me before men, him will I confess also before My Father which is in Heaven."

The whole experience was a revelation to me as a preacher. The same text outside of a revival atmosphere would not have produced the same results, but with the Holy Spirit's presence, the sinners were helpless. Glory to God!

ARABIAN SCHOOL OF THE HOLY SPIRIT

Throughout the history of the Church, a characteristic of many revivals is that the power of the Holy Spirit seems to be tangibly present. Many noticed this special atmosphere on the school compound even in Arabia. Two Muslims who delivered office supplies had no intentions of attending a revival meeting, nor did they suspect that such meetings were even taking place! Nevertheless, when their feet touched the compound, they fell down under the power of the Holy Spirit for more than a half hour. When they were able to stand on their feet again, they immediately requested Bibles.

During the services, the Holy Spirit imparted several visions: the glory of God hovering over that school, and His glory was being disseminated to the north, south, east, and west as the Lord's servants and handmaidens were equipped to be sent into the harvest fields of the Middle East and Asia. I saw the Spirit of the Lord loosening the Arabian "boot" of its inappropriately tied laces (cords of darkness). The glory cloud became a blackboard on which the hand of the Lord wrote, "School of the Holy Spirit in Arabia." I also saw the hand of God roll a black cloud off of the Arabian Peninsula.

Who would have possibly imagined that the Lord would start a revival in the midst of an Islamic country, but truly there was an open Heaven over that school!

REVIVAL IN THE GALILEE

Currently the Holy Spirit is moving in a new way in Israel in the Galilee. Some of the meetings continue past midnight. A man who was immobilized in bed from a heart condition was raised up when we prayed for him. Others suffering from Muslim folk curses were delivered and cancer patients set free from all symptoms of the disease.

A Muslim woman had been diagnosed with an incurable skin disease and was hospitalized in the Galilee. She experienced a recurring dream in which she was searching for Jesus. In her dreams she climbed a mountain looking for Jesus. Somebody said, "His throne is at the top of this mountain." She cried, "I don't want his chair—I want Him!" When finally she found Jesus in her dream, she fell down at His feet and worshipped Him. She woke up totally healed! This woman, a hairdresser, was anointed with oil by a young Arab pastor and regularly attends revival meetings as a testimony that Jesus is alive and still heals today. Seeking Muslims hungry for reality and truth pay for many of the meetings' ministry expenses.

These accounts are some of the Acts of the Holy Spirit in our day. *The Holy Spirit revivals in which I am so privileged to participate have given me faith to believe for revival anywhere and in some of the earth's most Gospel-resistant places! A genuine revival does not always consist of great crowds. Our great need is the manifest presence of the living Lord Jesus Christ!*

SUGGESTIONS FOR PRAYER

Pray therefore for the manifest presence of Jesus, which is the essence of revival!

Pray fervently for revival in the Muslim world, that the Lord will send faithful Bible teachers to strengthen the new believers—many of whom told me that they desire with all of their hearts to serve the Lord in full-time ministry. Truly the Lord has established a teaching center within the very citadels of the Middle East! Pray for more open heavens in the Middle East such as we have enjoyed.

Pray earnestly for dreams and visions to increase in the most unlikely places and to the most unlikely people and leaders (religious and political leaders). The apostle Paul was a very hostile religious leader and opponent of Christianity, yet his "Damascus Road" conversion, when he met Jesus in an open vision, changed him into the greatest evangelist who ever lived.

Our God's arm is not so short that it cannot save, and the Lord is communicating the glorious Gospel like streams in the desert in these

Last Days! There is undeniable evidence that the Holy Spirit is hovering over nations, and the awesome presence of Jesus is being manifested powerfully. God's Spirit is stirring not only in Muslims lands but in China, all over Africa, India, South America, in all the former Soviet states, and in nearly every nation on earth. Even in Islamic lands, ministries such as Teen Challenge have been allowed to establish Gospel-oriented drug programs, and CBN TV built one of the world's largest Gospel TV studios in the most populous Muslim country, Indonesia.

However, more than anything else, the greatest prayer need is for Jesus Christ to be manifested. Pray for the presence of Jesus Christ in the Middle East and in every nation, as happened in the Arabian revival.

The refreshing of the Holy Spirit and revelation of His manifest presence—not signs, wonders, and spiritual gifts—should exalt Jesus alone. The greatest revelation in the Last Days should be the glory and power of Christ.

Give us Jesus—the melting, healing, awesome presence of the Lord—more than anything else!

Finally, "Not unto us, O Lord, not unto us, but unto thy name give glory, for thy mercy, and for thy truth's sake" (Psalm 115:1).

GLOSSARY

ALLAH:	the god of Islam
CALIPH:	title given to Mohammed's successors
HADITH:	collection of the sayings and actions of Mohammed
HAJJI:	title given to a Muslim who has made the pilgrimage to Mecca, which is one of the five pillars of the Islamic religion
HAMAS:	Palestinian terrorist organization
IMAM:	in the hierarchies of Islam, a high religious official
INJIL:	the Gospels
INTIFADA:	Arabic word for "uprising."
ISLAM:	means "submission" and is a religion established by Mohammed with Allah as the object of worship
ISA/ISSA:	Islamic name for Jesus
JIHAD:	religious war, struggle
JINN:	in Muslim legend, a spirit believed to be capable of assuming human or animal form and exercising supernatural influence over people
KA'ABA:	house of Allah, a cubical building in Mecca. Pilgrims walk around this building and kiss the Black Stone meteorite. It is in the direction of this building and its stone that Muslims must bow and pray five times a day.
KORAN:	Islamic holy book
MINARET:	mosque prayer tower
MULLAH:	leader in a mosque, an Islamic priest
MUSLIM:	one who submits to Islam and recites its creed that "there is no god but Allah and Mohammed is his prophet"
RAMADAN:	the name of the month when Muslims fast, which is one of the five pillars of the Islamic religion
SHAZLI:	a sect of Muslims in Damascus; many believed in Jesus

SHIA/ SHI'ITE:	Muslim of this sect is a follower of Ali, one of the successors of Mohammed
SUFI:	a mystical Muslim very susceptible to dreams and visions
SUNNI:	a Muslim who honors Omar as Mohammed's successor
SURA:	a chapter in the Koran

ABOUT THE AUTHOR

Evangelist Christine Darg discovered that the supernatural, and not mere theological argumentation, is a major key to win the Muslim world to Christ. She explains why the Lord is favoring the Middle East in an unprecedented move of the Holy Spirit and how you can be a part of it through prayer, dream interpretation, and friendship evangelism.

Islamic terrorism may dominate headlines, but hot news behind the scenes is that the risen Lord Jesus is visiting Muslims through dreams and visions. Christine Darg heard the voice of God in a dream say, "Go!" to an Arabian city where the Holy Spirit was moving in revival. She chronicles outstanding dreams and visions in this current move of God, and also shares startling visions she herself has experienced in the Middle East and throughout the world.

In remarkable ways and on a seemingly unprecedented scale in fulfillment of Bible prophecy (Acts 1:3), the Lord is showing Himself alive!

Miracles Among Muslims is an unexaggerated account of signs and wonders because Jesus continues to be "the same yesterday, today and forever" (Hebrews 13:8).

God is pouring out His Spirit in the dry places before the Lord's return. He is also fulfilling His ancient promise to Abraham that

Ishmael might live! Dreams and visions are prophesied to be primary characteristics of the end-time revival, and they are definitely some of the main ways that the Lord is communicating the Gospel to the children of Abraham:

> *And it shall come to pass afterward, that I will pour out my spirit upon all flesh; and your sons and your daughters shall prophesy, your old men shall dream dreams, your young men shall see visions* (Joel 2:28).

Although dreams may play a relatively insignificant role in the conversions of most Westerners, over one-fourth of believers surveyed in the Islamic world stated emphatically that dreams and visions were key in drawing them to Christ and sustained them through difficult times.

CONTACT THE AUTHOR

Christine Darg would appreciate communicating with you by e-mail concerning any questions that you may have as a result of reading *Miracles Among Muslims*. Perhaps you've experienced a dream or a vision that you would like to share with her.

She can be contacted via e-mail at:
info@exploits.tv.
exploitsministry@mac.com

The text of this volume is available in Arabic at
www.jesusvisions.org

Additional copies of this book and other book titles from DESTINY IMAGE EUROPE are available at your local bookstore.

We are adding new titles every month!

To view our complete catalog online, visit us at:
www.eurodestinyimage.com

Send a request for a catalog to:

Via Acquacorrente, 6
65123 - Pescara - ITALY
Tel. +39 085 4716623 - Fax +39 085 4716622

"Changing the world, one book at a time!"

Are you an author?

Do you have a "today" God-given message?

CONTACT US

We will be happy to review your manuscript for a possible publishing:

publisher@eurodestinyimage.com